I Don't Know if it Happened This Way

. . .

Gary J. Buehler

I Don't Know if it Happened This Way

Copyright © 2022

by Gary J. Buehler

Cover & book design by Lucretia Alejandre

Published by

New Education Press

www.NewEducationPress.com

ISBN: 978-1-932842-89-0 — $ 17.95

Printed in the United States of America

dedicated to

the love of my life | *Charlotte*

and our children | *Tonja, Tammy,* and *Todd*

and their children | *Kyle, Eliza, Hanna* and *Gavin*

with special thanks to
members of our writing groups

Paul Arndt, Deborah Doolittle Arndt, Rae-Ellen Kavey, MD

Melanie Krebs, Joani Pedzich and Wayne VanderByl, JD

advisors, reviewers,
copy editor, and publisher

Copy Editor | Rae-Ellen Kavey, MD

Publisher | Steven Swerdfeger, PhD

Designer | Lucretia Alejandre

Review | Jim Komeliusen

and all members of the

writing groups

Table of Contents

1 — A QUICK GLANCE IN THE MIRROR...1

2 — 1:13 AM, 1959, BIG SPRING, TEXAS...7

3 — CLOSE ONE 15

4 — ANOTHER FISH STORY...21

5 — LIQUOR DOES STRANGE THINGS TO MEN'S MINDS
AND PERHAPS THEIR EGOS 27

6 — MEASURE TWICE 31

7 — WHERE'S THE OWNER?..37

8 — THE SECRET FISHING HOLE IN MUNSEN 45

9 — JOHNNY 53

10 — MOTHER ANN MEETS LONG JOHN SILVER......................59

11 — FOXHOLE RADIO 63

12 — THE BET..69

13 — I QUIT 73

14 — WONDERING 79

15 — FINE WHISKY AND WINE 85

16 — CHRISTMAS KITCHEN MEMORIES 91

17 — JOHANNA..95

18 — THE ELUSIVE CUP...105

19 — GEORGE'S HAM SANDWICH...109

20 — JUST ONE LITTLE BOTTLE
WAS ALL THAT WAS NEEDED...113

21 — CLOVERINE 117

22 — THE BIG TOE 123

23 — WHAT I WILL MISS 127

24 — PERHAPS WE JUST REFLECT 129

25 — 1940 AND TODAY 135

26 — CAN YOU SEE THE OTHER SIDE OF THE MOON?...........139

27 — CONTEMPLATE...141

28 — THE PENGUIN AND THE CARDBOARD BOX CAPER 143

29 — RED SHIRT AND HIS DRUMS 149

30 — THE CAT, PARAKEET, AND FRUIT CAKE 157

31 — THE WEDDING...163

32 — A HORSE BY ANY OTHER NAME... 167

33 — WEARING OF THE GREEN..171

34 — IF A LITTLE IS GOOD..173

35 — SHE WAS A BEAUTY
AND IT WAS MY BIRTHDAY AFTER ALL............................179

36 — WOVEN TAPESTRY...185

Prologue

If you are you curious about the title... then we may have something in common!

My memoir published in 2018 was written at the request of one of our daughters who wanted me to write down all my childhood stories that I shared with the family on car rides, at our cabin, or at family gatherings around the holidays. That's how this all started after my third retirement. It was a joy to undertake the challenge, and after publication, the feedback over the following months and intervening years has been a morale and ego-booster, motivating me to attempt to record some more of these tales. Accolades were not my original motivation for putting pen to paper, they simply turned out to be a wonderful bonus.

As for the title of this book, it was referenced obliquely in my first book. I mentioned theologian, Dr. Marcus J. Borg, in the Prologue of my memoir, **An American Story.** When Dr. Marcus was about to begin a lecture or a sermon based on the New Testament and the parables contained therein, he usually began with the statement, "Now I don't know if it happened this way or not, but I know these stories to be true..." This kind of grabs your attention a bit and tests your listening, reading, and thinking skills, doesn't it?

None of these stories in this edition are biblical or compare, by any stretch of the imagination, to the parables in the Bible, nor are they intended to test your beliefs in any way. If anything, they are there to test my ability as a storyteller, nothing more, nothing less.

Since my first book of stories was fun to put together, I thought I'd try writing a few more short ones and perhaps one or two of these yet-to-be-told tales wound up with a few embellishments. Your challenge, as the reader, is to sift through the following stories and try to determine if you can detect any malarkey. Someone who has written many books once told me, "Only write about something you know."

I tried to do just that with the realization that at my advanced age, not only are my eyes growing dimmer, but so are the distant memories, not to mention the rest of the structures that hold a person up and assist them in moving forward. Forgive me, as I'm doing the best I can under the circumstances of more than four scores plus one or two or more.

So, there you have it. These are tales of some experiences I've had, enjoyed, learned from, and been embarrassed by. I leave you with two challenges: one, to see if you can spot any malarkey, and two, try to figure out the title. Neither should be a difficult challenge.

And please, enjoy the lighthearted reading of these tales as,

I don't know if it happened this way . . .

A Quick Glance in the Mirror

Bonnie was cute and she knew it. All the boys knew it too. Her mom was single, raising her alone in a small town near the state line. It wasn't easy but sometimes, when she was in a good mood and hadn't had too much to drink, she hugged her girl and called her Bonnie Bell, a small sign of affection. All the boys noticed Bonnie whenever she came to town with her mom to shop at the Food Mart, and in the halls and classes at school. She had beautiful bright green eyes and long, light brown hair; she was tall and carried herself as if she owned the very real estate she walked on. Her lips were perfect, drawn up just a bit at the corners, like the Mona Lisa — her smile could almost be mistaken for a smirk. When the boys were alone and talked about the girls in school, they all referred to her as BB with a touch of adoration in their voices.

In high school, the boys tripped over their own feet walking down the hall or into the cafeteria while staring at Bonnie, smitten just to be in her commanding presence. Jimmy James was in love with her from the first time she walked into his junior high English class. Jimmy's father owned the body shop in town and he worked with him during the summers and after school. By the time he was 16, Jimmy had his license and his own car — the coolest custom car and one of the fastest cars in the county. It was painted a deep metallic cherry red with gold flake and shone like a diamond in the sun. As a matter of fact, Jimmy's Mercury was as nice as any of the custom cars in the whole state of California, the birthplace and bedrock of custom cars.

Bonnie liked Jimmy and his Mercury. But which was higher on her list, Jimmy or the car? This question was endlessly debated when the guys talked at parties, when they were alone, and every time they drove out to the quarry to drink beer and raise hell. Whenever the red and gold Mercury was spotted around town, you could be sure Bonnie Bell was by Jimmy's side, riding shotgun.

There was never a question of who Jimmy was taking to the senior prom and never any question who was going to be elected prom queen. Prom King was another subject, open to endless conjecture — and politics, friendships, and envy being what they are, it was still an open question until all the ballots were counted. In the end, the Mercury carried the king and queen out for the rest of the night after the prom was over. Jimmy and Bonnie were the perfect royal couple, holding court that night at the dance.

Graduation arrived quicker than a greased pig escaping the barnyard. Jimmy settled into a full-time position, six days a week at the body shop. Bonnie Bell wanted more time with Jimmy — and more time riding in the Mercury on those summer days after graduation, but that was something Jimmy's full-time job did not allow. One day, Bonnie disappeared from town. Her mom said she'd just gotten up, packed a suitcase and walked out of the house saying, "Ma, I'll call you soon and let you know where I'm at when I get there." But the call never came and Bonnie's mother sank deeper and deeper into depression, drowning her sorrows and the missing piece of her heart.

Years passed. Never a word was heard from Bonnie by her mother or Jimmy, the King of the Prom. Jimmy's dad passed away and Jimmy took over the business. Success and money came his way — with his work ethic and good business sense, he was even able to expand the shop. Through business associates, word was passed along to Jimmy about a possible opportunity in Tennessee. A major auto body shop was for sale due to the death of the owner and the estate's lawyer was trying to maximize the value of the business and property. Tired of the snow and cold, Jimmy decided to take a trip south to examine the new opportunity. On arrival, Mort Sawyer, the attorney for the estate, met him at the airport and dropped him at his motel, telling him he'd pick him up for dinner at 6:00 p.m.

Dinner at the steakhouse was wonderful. Chit chat included some basic numbers for the business and an agreement to meet the next day for breakfast and then for a tour of the facility. After dessert, Mort suggested a night cap, telling Jimmy, "I know this perfect place that I think you'll like, it's called the Diamond." The bar was an upscale nightclub in the downtown area. A hostess checked their jackets and walked them to the beautiful solid walnut bar which extended the full length of the building. Each glass shelf was softly lit and offerings consisted of every imaginable crystal bottle of spirits anyone had ever even dreamed of ordering. Mort placed an order for a 25-year-old bottle of scotch from the top shelf, along with two glasses.

Jimmy looked into the mirror on the wall behind the glass bar shelves and saw a painting in the reflection of the wall behind where they were seated. He felt a rush and his heart quickened. He turned in his chair and then walked over to view it clearly, without the liquor bottles on the shelves in the way. There on the wall was an oil painting in a golden frame of a stunningly beautiful young woman with a large diamond necklace resting on her bosom. Blood rushed to Jimmy's face as emotions raced through his mind and body.

Jimmy: "Who is the lady in the painting?"

Mort: "That's the owner, Constance Swartz. Notice the
                diamonds — that necklace was an extraordinary gift to
                her from one of her many... friends... from a long time
                ago. Actually, it was quite a while before, when a certain
                individual asked her to marry him. That special lady,
                Ms. Swartz, owns this building, this bar, the whole block
                and perhaps even the whole town. Understand what I'm
                saying and where I'm coming from? Sort of like Bonnie
                and Clyde, if you get my drift?"

Jimmy: "Yeah... How long has she been living here? How long
                has she owned this bar?"

Mort: "I'd guess 20 years or so. I've been coming here for at
                least that long. The Rotary meets here every Tuesday,
                upstairs. They have an excellent lunch menu. The
                Downtown Business Council also holds all their
                meetings here."

Jimmy: "Really!"

Mort: "Yeah...really. And one other important thing — she's
                married to the mayor."

Jimmy: "You don't say, the Mayor! Does she ever come in
                here?"

Mort: "Not anymore. She used to manage the business here herself but now she has Hank managing this place, the department store next door, and the hardware store down the street. The Mayor is in here all the time. Since she's been married, maybe 15 years or so, Ms. Swartz spends all her time doing charity work — she's on the Board of the Art Museum, the Philharmonic, and the Garden Club."

Jimmy: "Why does the painting stay up on the wall? I'd think the Mayor would be upset with everyone staring at this... suggestive painting of his wife, perhaps making rude comments, or... you know what I mean. It could cause all kinds of problems."

Mort: "The Mayor is pretty liberal and likes to be kind of a showboat. Besides, I've heard him say more than once, 'If you got it, it's OK to flaunt it!'"

Jimmy: "I can't believe that."

Mort: "Well, the Mayor runs everything in this town, and I mean EVERYTHING! So there's no chance of anyone ever saying anything off key about the painting, his wife, or for that matter, anything about him at all. End of story!"

Jimmy: "I'm pretty sure I knew the Mayor's wife a long time ago when she was much younger."

Mort: "You don't say."

Jimmy:	"Yes, really, I'm not kidding. I knew her very well!"
Mort:	"Well son, you best keep that ALL to yourself... if you know what's good for you. Drink up and let's get the hell out of here. End of the line for us tonight... tomorrow's another day, let's get our business done so we can wrap up this deal and you can get back home up north. I know you know a good deal when you see one and I'm here to help you close it. By the way, if this works out the way I think it's going to work out, let me ask you this... will you and your family be moving here or will you have one of your managers run it for you? I should have asked you first if you're married and if you have a family. Either way, this is a pretty nice town but you really need to have the mayor on your side if you want to do any kind of business hereabouts."
Jimmy:	"How about you take me back to the motel now and let me sleep on this."

1:13 am, 1959, Big Spring, Texas

Let's see your license and registration.

"I need to get them out of the glove compartment."

Keep one hand on the steering wheel and get your papers with your other hand. You sit right there and don't move. What's this red sticker on your windshield from the crossing at the bridge into Mexico? What's that bottle I see in your glove box? Slowly, hand it over here to me. What's this? Where did you get this?

"It's No Doz."

Where did you get this... Mexico? These are drugs, and they're not legal in Texas.

"No officer, I bought them in Daw's Drug Store in Rochester."

Rochester?

"Yes, Rochester, New York."

Never heard of Daw's or No Doz and there's no Daw's stores in Big Spring. I think you're smuggling drugs. We're gonna search your car. Get out and get in the back seat of the patrol car.

It felt like many miles to the station, and I was shaking terribly, with tears streaming down my face as we entered the parking lot behind police headquarters.

OK, we're here. Get out and come with me.

I was put in a locked room with no windows, just a table and chair. After what seemed like hours, the officer came back and told me to follow him. We walked down several miles of halls to a room filled with desks, only one of which was occupied. I was led to that desk. I guessed that the suit behind the desk was a detective.

I picked this kid up out on the expressway doing 70 in the 35-mph zone. Here's a bottle of drugs I found in his glove box. I was suspicious because he's been into Mexico and he wasn't even smart enough to remove the entry sticker from his windshield. I'm having his car towed to the garage for a complete search. I'm pretty sure we'll find more drugs in the car. He's all yours.

Well son, what do you have to say for yourself?

"I'm on a trip around the country. I'm sorry about speeding. I never saw the reduced speed limit. All the signs for miles read 70 mph. I guess I missed the city speed limit sign."

What were you doing in Mexico?

"I just wanted to see Mexico."

You just wanted to see Mexico?

"Yes! And I wanted to tell my friends back home that I had visited Mexico on my trip. That's why I left the visa sticker on the windshield."

What were you doing before you went to Mexico?

"I was in Carlsbad, California with my aunt and uncle for a couple of weeks."

How did you get to Carlsbad from New York?

"I drove across the country and out to Orcas Island in Washington to visit another aunt and uncle and stayed there for a week. Then I drove down to my aunt's place in California because I wanted to see all of Washington and Oregon on the way down the coast."

Why did you come to Texas and what are you doing here? Who are you going to see in Texas? "No one, I'm on my way to Florida."

Florida? You told the Officer you were from New York. Florida's not on the way to New York from California or Texas!

"Yes, I did tell him I was from New York. I am from New York — Rochester, New York."

Your story just doesn't add up. Why don't you tell me the truth about what you've been up to and why you are on the run?

"I'm not on the run!"

Why are you going to Florida?

"I'm going to St. Augustine to visit family friends and stay with them for a week or so."

Family friends? Who would that be?

"Bill Brosch. He has a Gulf station that he operates there. He used to live in Rochester and he operated a Gulf station there and I hung out at the station a lot. Besides, he's a friend of the family. Also, he moved his family to Florida because he didn't like the winters and I want to surprise him and stop in and say 'Hi.'"

Just stop in and surprise him? Boy, you can tell some tall tales. You expect me to believe all this bullcrap?

"I'm telling you the TRUTH!"

Who can I call to verify if what you're telling me has any truth to it at all?

"You can call my mother or my grandmother in Greece, New York."

You told me you were from Rochester and now you're telling me you're from Greece? Are you sure you're not from Mars?

"Greece is a suburb of Rochester."

OK kid. What's your mother's phone number?

"Greenwood (GR) 8-0863."

Is that your mother's number or your grandmother's number?

"It's both, but my mother might not be home, just my grandmother."

The detective stares at me and slowly dials the number and waits, listens, and then hangs the phone up in the cradle.

Nice try, bud. The operator says that number you just gave me doesn't work. It is no longer a working number. Why don't you just come clean and tell me the whole story of why you're in trouble, on the run, and dealing drugs? It will be easier on you later if you come clean now.

"I AM telling the truth. There is NO story. Can I try making the phone call myself?"

You get to make just ONE call and then you are going to jail if I can't verify all these stories.

The detective picks up the phone. He dials the operator and requests that this call be put through to New York via long distance. Between tears and trying to dial with my arms, hands,

and fingers shaking and my legs trembling, I try hard to carefully dial; GR 8 - 0-8-6-3. The phone rings once.

This is the operator... the number you are calling is no longer valid.

I hand the phone back to the detective in tears.

OK, I'm not wasting any more time with you bud. Come with me.

We walk down several more corridors to the intake desk at the jail.

Joe, this guy gets locked up tonight. I'll talk to him tomorrow when I come in for my shift. He's scared out of his wits as you can see, so you better keep him alone by himself tonight. Try 113 if it's open.

OK kid, empty your pockets on the counter. Take the shoelaces out of your shoes. Give me your belt. I'm putting your $300 in travelers checks and $108 in cash into this envelope. You seal it and sign your name here. Your wallet, belt, shoelaces, change, and pocketknife go in this envelope. Leave it on the counter and come with me.

I'm led through two sets of locked doors to a single room and the guard slides the door locked behind me. I had never felt so alone or scared in my entire life. I also had to urinate badly. I sat on the cot and just cried. Gradually the tears began to slow down and the shaking ebbed a bit, just a bit, and then my muscles begin to ache. They ached like I had walked a thousand miles and lifted hundreds of pounds of weight for hours on end. Finally, overcome with tiredness, I fell asleep.

A guard returns and wakes me up. I have no idea what time it is or even if it's day or night. He tells me to follow him. We snake our way through miles of corridors and I am suddenly back in the room with the desks, all now occupied. I'm marched back to stand in front of the same detective I had spoken to the night before.

I contacted the Rochester Police Department and then the Greece Police Department, and they confirm your story. The Greece Police gave me your grandmother's phone number. I called and spoke with her. Your grandmother said the last she heard from you was a postcard mailed from you to her. She said you wrote that you were with the Guilford's in Carlsbad, California. She also said she had received a postcard from you several weeks before when you were with other

Guilford's on Orcas Island in Washington. Grandma didn't know anything about Mexico. I also called Daw's Drugs and they confirmed they sell No Doz over the counter and it is legal in New York. The Greece Police told me the phone system in Greece had been converted to automatic dialing and the old numbers were no longer in use. Here is your grandmother's new phone number. Don't lose that piece of paper, son. Maybe you need to call her soon. Here, open this and count your money. Sign here that you have received all your money back. Take this other envelope and follow me.

We walk through another few miles of corridors and two sets of doors, out to the parking lot, and right there sits my car. Without a word, the detective turns around and leaves me standing there. My pants are almost falling down and I don't have shoelaces in my shoes. I open the envelope and put myself back together. Then I go over to check out my car. The interior has been completely torn apart. The tire in the trunk has been taken off the rim. Under the hood, the air clearer has been removed from the carburetor. I turn around and find my way back to the detective.

"I checked my car and it's all been torn apart. The spare tire was dismounted from the rim and I need it put back together. Can you tell the garage guys to fix the tire for me?"

Tell you what, son, get the hell out of here right now and don't look back. Never come back here again. Consider yourself lucky you didn't get a speeding ticket. Now, get outta here!

* * * * * * * *

Decades pass. Just two years ago, I was driving cross country with my wife Charlotte, returning home from California on the interstate and I notice the sign: Big Spring, Speed Limit, 35 mph.

"You know, hon, I spent a night in jail right here in Big Spring on my trip around the states when you were in school at Houghton. Remember the map you had on your wall in the dorm and the pins you stuck in all the places you received postcards from?"

"Yes, I remember and I remember that whole story. I have just one question: are you going 35?"

I Don't Know if it Happened This Way . . .

Close One

Saturday night, date night and Judy was waiting! This particular February evening was especially cold with the mercury in the thermometer on the wall of the back porch holding at -12 degrees. As Matt walked through the snow to his old Ford in the driveway, his boots made the crunchy, squeaking sound they always made when it was really cold. As he opened the driver's door, a mass of snow on the roof and door window slid off, covering his bare hands and head in an avalanche of white mist. He brushed a pile of the fluffy stuff off the seat and slid in behind the wheel, slamming the door behind him and reaching for the key in the ignition. The starter moaned as it turned the engine over slowly — the old 6-volt battery was taxed to its maximum.

"Judy is waiting." Matt muttered under his breath. "Come on baby... start for me just this once!" The engine sputtered to life for a moment, then quit.

"Damn!" Once more Matt hit the starter button and held it in, pumping the gas pedal up and down until the engine finally roared to life. He let it warm up before turning on the wipers to clear the windshield but the blades thudded back and forth without even beginning to budge the heavy, frozen accumulation. He rushed back to the kitchen to retrieve his mom's broom and swept off the windows, doors and hood as fast as he could.

"Damn! Already 15 minutes late to pick up Judy."

Backing out of the driveway, he got stuck in the snowbank left by the road plow. Back he went, this time to the garage for the snow shovel. After 15 minutes of hard digging, he was finally able to back into the roadway. The drive to Judy's was horrendous over streets covered in deep snow with tired tires that had seen many miles and better days. Determined not to miss his date, he got up a head of steam and tried to pull into Judy's driveway — and he almost made it. He ran to the house for her dad's snow shovel — another 15 minutes of digging and they were finally on their way.

By then, it was 8:15 — Judy had to be home by ten and it was already too late to make the Elvis movie, so they decided to just drive around town as a challenge, to see if they could avoid getting stuck again, and maybe find the malt shop open for a bite to eat. With the snow shovel tucked behind the front seat and Matt with no fear of deep snow driving, it seemed like a good plan.

They made it downtown and over to the bowling alley to see if any of their friends might be there on this snowy night. They were just pulling up in front of the main entrance to the building when two big guys in overcoats and fedora hats came marching out the front door, dragging a teenager between them. He was locked arm-in-arm with these two big bozos, one on each side. They marched him to a Chevy sedan parked at the curb, pushed him into the back seat, then jumped into the front seat and took off down the street.

"Judy, did you see THAT!?"

"Matt, what the heck is going on?"

"I think they are kidnapping that kid."

"Matt, let's get out of here."

"Judy, we can't, we've gotta help that kid."

"OK, OK. Let's stop some place and call the cops."

"Judy, did you get the plate number of the sedan? I know, I know — of course you couldn't. It was all covered with snow."

"Matt! Let's just go and find a cop car or a pay phone and report this and let them take care of it."

"Judy, they're getting away, I don't know what they're going to do to that kid or where they're taking him. We need to follow them."

"Are you crazy?"

"Judy, don't worry, we'll just tail them to see where they are going. Maybe you can see their license plate and then we'll call the police and report all this."

The old Ford with the balding tires followed the sedan and finally caught up at the next intersection. As soon as they pulled up, the sedan made a U-turn and started back up the same street towards the bowling hall. Even though the light was red by the time he reached it, Matt threw the car into a U-turn and raced after them. He was two or three car lengths behind the sedan when it started to slow down. Judy told Matt that she thought they had been spotted. Sure enough, the sedan pulled over to the curb and stopped. Matt kept going and passed right by them. The sedan then pulled out behind them and started flashing its lights. Judy told Matt that she thought they wanted them to pull over and stop. Matt told Judy that she was crazy because there was no way he was going to stop because he didn't know what they'd do to them.

"Judy, we are witnesses and they got a kid in their back seat, what will they do to us? This is serious, that kid is in danger and so are we. We need to call the cops like right now! Look for a cop car. They could kill us because we witnessed the whole thing. I'm scared as _____."

Matt kept trying to pull away but the snow and the tires on his car held them back. The sedan was right behind them, flashing its headlights on and off. Suddenly, the sedan was right alongside their car. The passenger-side window was down and one big guy was half hanging out, hollering for him to pull over and stop. He could see the guy was holding something in his hand but Matt kept going. Then he noticed the guy had a gun in his other hand and was shouting for him to pull over. No way was he going to stop now with these two guys chasing him with a gun! But both traffic lanes were stopped ahead for a traffic light and now Matt was boxed in with cars behind and ahead of him and the guys in the other car alongside — there was nowhere to go. The sedan stopped close to Matt's Ford and both big guys jumped out, one running to Matt's side of the car and the other over by Judy.

It was then and only then that Matt not only saw the gun was pointed at the ground but also recognized the badge in the guy's other hand. He glanced over at Judy who was in tears with the other guy screaming for her to roll down the window. He had the same type of badge in his hand but thank God he didn't have a gun!

"What the hell do you kids think you are doing following us? Do you know that kid in the back seat? Is he a friend of yours?"
"No! We thought you were kidnapping him from the bowling hall."
"We arrested him for disorderly conduct and we were taking him to the station. Let's see your driver's license. Who is that girl with you? Let's see some identification for her."

After ordering Matt not to move the car or get out, the guy with the gun returned to the Chevy sedan — now identified as a police car. The other guy stayed by Judy's window asking her one question after another. After what felt like at least an hour, the guy in the Chevy finally returned, handed Matt his license and told him in a most unpleasant way to mind his own business from now on.

There was quiet in the car as Matt drove off. He glanced at his watch — quarter to ten, just enough time to get Judy home before her curfew. Judy didn't seem to mind that at all.

Back home, Matt's legs were still shaking hours later. Try as he might, he could not digest this crazy evening and figure out exactly where the train left the tracks.

* * * * * * * *

Matt and Judy were married the following summer. Although they often talk about their early dating years, they almost never share the story of this particular date with anyone else. But the memory remains and the heart beats just a bit faster thinking of that snowy evening in February of 1969.

Another Fish Story

Some people talk way too much! Case in point: over Christmas break in the early 1960's, I was a married college student with no money for tuition for the looming second semester. Everybody knew I loved cars and that was where a unique opportunity presented itself. You see, there was one very beautiful 1962 "bubble top" Super Sport Chevy in our area, well known as both a show car and a very fast race car — but the owner didn't know when to keep his mouth shut. As the story emerged, it seemed a perfect recipe was at play: all one had to do was add a large ego, a pinch of bragging and plenty of booze until all friends were well saturated — bake for a few hours and we'd have this consummate, devious opportunity. And this is pretty much how it happened...

"Hey, did you hear they found Bob's perfect, cherry Chevy in the canal?"

"No way!"

"Yeah, last week when they drained the canal for the winter someone spotted the caved-in roof of a car and called the cops."

"How'd the top get pushed in? Flipped over when it went in?"

"Nah, I don't think so; my guess is that a barge hit it when it was buried in the water. The canal is pretty shallow out by Clinton Avenue where they pulled it out."

"The Democrat and Chronicle had a picture of the car being towed out of the canal. Then yesterday, I saw it sitting out in front of the junk yard on West Henrietta Road."

"What kind of shape is it in?"

"Looks okay other than the top being flattened. All the windows are rolled down and the windshield and rear window aren't even cracked."

"I wonder how Bob feels now that they found his precious car?"

"That's what's so interesting about this whole thing... you know, he reported it being stolen back in October and the insurance company settled and gave him a big check."

"Yeah...?"

"Well, here's the thing... Bob was hanging out at McGinty's with his buddies last Saturday and the guys were on his case about the picture of the bubble top being pulled out of the canal. Bob was bragging that he was making out like a bandit. Not only getting his car back but he was going to sell all the racing parts from it and make a killing."

"How is that even possible?"

"He told everyone that he had contacted the insurance company and that he was buying the car back for $200. If anyone wanted the race engine, 4-speed and Hurst shifter, the American magnesium racing wheels with new tires, the fuel injection unit, or the positraction unit and 4:11 gears, they should get in touch with him. He said he'll sell all the parts including the engine for a great price."

"I heard someone pointed out that the engine would be ruined because of sitting in the water for so long, and he told him, no... that he filled the cylinders and injection unit with oil before it went into the canal and everything would be perfectly protected from rusting. He said it was all part of the plan."

First thing Monday morning I drove out to the junk yard and there was the Chevy, front and center behind the fence, looking just as described. The guy in the office told me that the insurance company was holding an auction and the car would be released to the highest bidder — he even gave me the name of the insurance company. Over the phone, the secretary at the insurance company told me it was a sealed bidding process closing at 1:00pm that day. I raced downtown, found the office and submitted a sealed written bid for $201, right before the deadline. My plan was falling right into place. The next morning the insurance company let me know I was the successful bidder — first stage of the mission accomplished.

The second stage was a little more complicated. The car had to be removed by Saturday so the next day, a friend and I arrived to tow it back to the garage in my apartment complex. We hooked the tow bar to the Chevy but the rear wheels just would not turn. After quite some time in the freezing cold, it finally dawned on us that the rear end gears in the housing had filled up with water in the canal, and the water had turned to ice. We unhooked the car and drove back to the garage, fetched my set of torches and then heated the rear end to melt the ice. It worked! It was a long day but we finally got the car back to my garage and pushed it in, jacked it up, and turned on the kerosene space heater to warm the work space up a bit.

The third stage was a lot of hard work. First, I spent several days taking out the engine, transmission, positraction, and the wheels — a hideous, muddy process. I lugged the parts over to my parent's home and in the basement, cleaned each one by scrubbing off the mud and silt that covered every surface. I removed the heads from the engine to inspect the cylinders and pistons and although they were also covered with muddy silt, underneath there was no hint of rust. So far, so good!

After placing an ad in the newspaper, I sold all the parts I had removed from the car — as if by magic, there was just enough money for my spring semester's tuition. I even had a surprise bonus. Lucky for me, it seems some people do talk too much! Not only did I win the bid on the car at auction, but somehow, word got around about the rescued 1962 Chevy. A body shop owner called and wanted to know if I would sell the front clip as they were repairing the same make of car with front end damage. He wanted the whole front clip including the fenders, the hood, the grill and the bumper. I agreed to sell if the shop guys would come to my garage and remove it all themselves, and also tow the remaining body without wheels to the junk yard. And that's how I ended up with an extra $200 just in time to return to school.

This may all sound like a lucky and winning adventure. In many ways, it was. But let me assure you it wasn't all that wonderful. As I lay under the car on sheets of cardboard, working to remove the transmission, motor mounts, drive shaft and the rear positraction unit, melting water dripped all over me. Ice cold water just showered down, covering my face, my hair, my clothes — even the cardboard was soaked. And the longer I worked, the worse it smelled. Finally, just before the body shop towed the remains of the car away, we decided to open the trunk to see if there was anything of value in it. There wasn't. However, the trunk did contain one big block of ice with dead fish still frozen in it.

I guess the fish had somehow gotten trapped in the trunk, probably swimming through the loose back seat. As I worked under the car with the space heater on, the ice melted providing me with that stinky shower. So much for having fun...Some people talk too much... perhaps even me for telling this story. As for Bob, the original owner and builder of a once beautiful car, I still wonder how he felt about his plan, the failed sealed bid and how he lost out on such a sure thing!

I Don't Know if it Happened This Way . . .

Liquor Does Strange Things to Men's Minds and Perhaps Their Egos

Before cell phones existed, there was no 911 to call. Your only option was to find a public pay phone and deposit a dime just to ask an operator for help. Drunk driving didn't seem to be the issue it is today: if a driver was stopped because of weaving back and forth in the road or driving too fast or too slow, the police would call a taxi or maybe even drop the person off at home. Used cars were fairly easy to find through ads in the local newspapers. There was even a period of time when a worn-out car wasn't worth trading in for a new one and many folks just wanted to get it out of their garage. It was during this era that as a teenager, I searched the want ads and finally found an old, but well-preserved 1949 Plymouth for which I paid the grand total of $45.

I enjoyed that car from the moment I brought it home. A few weeks into our partnership, the unbelievable happened, very late on a Saturday evening. I was in the middle of an intersection proceeding to turn left when the driver of a new Pontiac drove right through the red light into the rear of my car. My old Plymouth was built like a tank, but the front end of the Pontiac folded up like a piece of tissue paper. The twisted bumper was bent back into the radiator and antifreeze and coolant were pouring out onto the road. On the driver's side, the fender was pushed back into the driver's door so the driver had to crawl out via the passenger's door. My old Plymouth had a scratched and dented bumper and a dent in the rear fender, but was really none the worse for wear, as the saying goes.

The driver of the other vehicle, dressed in a suit and tie, came screaming at me, howling, "Do you know who I am?" I did not and said so. This was not helpful — he was even more upset, hollering, "Move your car out of the intersection over there by the curb." I remembered my uncle telling me once, "If you have an accident, don't move your car until the police arrive and they'll tell you to move it if they want it moved." With this in mind, I simply said, "I'm not moving my car." To which he replied, "Move your car now, do you know who I am?" His breath was heavy with the undeniable smell of alcohol and a saliva-soaked, unlit cigar was clenched tightly between his teeth.

He stormed back to his car and managed with considerable difficulty to get it started and moved to the curb, leaving a rivulet of steaming radiator fluid pooling in the street. I was now standing by my car and he came screaming back again, shouting, "Let's see your license." I responded with a slight smirk, "I don't have one." I could see the redness in his face deepening to the color of ruby. The smell of liquor on his breath was so strong that I didn't even notice the smell of the cigar. I could see he was totally out of control so I decided to have a little more fun. He shouted again, "Let me see your registration and insurance card right now so I can write down your information." I replied, "I don't have a registration card and I have no insurance." With this, the veins in his forehead bulged out like fingers under a thin sheet, as if they were ready to burst.

Just then, a patrol car pulled up behind my car and turned on its flashing red lights. The officer walked over to the other driver who was now standing by his car. I could easily hear what he was shouting, "That kid doesn't have a license, no registration, and no insurance and he ran into me and never stopped for the red light!" The policeman talked for a while and the driver calmed down a bit. I could no longer hear what he was saying, but he was still pointing to my car in the middle of the intersection and then at the traffic light and then back at the severely damaged front end of his car.

I had the suspicious feeling that the cop knew who he was, without him shouting, "Do you know who I am?" They talked for a long time which gave me time to prepare. Finally, the cop opened up the passenger door of the patrol car and had him sit down in the front seat. The officer then walked over to me, "Can I see your driver's license?" I handed it to him. He inspected it carefully, noting that it was a chauffeur's license. He asked me why and I told him that I drove a truck for a lumber company. He then asked, "May I see your registration and insurance card?" to which I replied, "Yes, sir, officer!" He walked back to the patrol car and sat there a long time. Returning to my car, which was still in the middle of the intersection, he handed back all my paperwork and said, "How is your car? Do you need a tow truck?" I assured him my car was fine. He told me I could file the accident with my insurance company and then said, "You are free to go. Drive safely."

I never did find out who the other driver was. I didn't recognize his name on the paper the policeman gave me... but I guess the guy who ran into me thought that I should have known him. Go figure...

Measure Twice

Bucky Buchanan drove a brand new 1953 shiny black Cadillac and was the only person I knew of that was wealthy enough to own one. Although I had never met him, he was already a legend in my mind when early one Saturday, my uncle asked if I wanted to go with him to the construction site where he was building a new house. I had nothing else planned for this particular Saturday so I jumped at the opportunity and we were off at seven o'clock in the morning.

I admired my uncle. He was a WWII veteran and an entrepreneur who had, among other things, built his own motorhome in which he traveled the US and even explored Mexico. He also built and then managed a Texaco gas station. He was an excellent mechanic and ran a very successful business. He had now decided to build his own home.

We pulled into the freshly cleared and bulldozed lot and there sat the beautiful, spotless Cadillac DeVille sedan. And inside sat Mr. Buchanan, apparently waiting for us to arrive. As we pulled into the lot, the driver's door swung open and he emerged: a short and very trim older man. He walked to the back, opened the trunk and pulled out a pair of bibbed overalls which he carefully put on over the pants and shirt he was wearing, before coming over to where we were standing. He bid us 'Good Morning' and reached for the cup of coffee from the thermos my uncle had brought from home.

"Gary, this is Mr. Buchanan," my uncle said introducing me.

"Glad to meet you son. You can call me Bucky."

"Glad to meet you, Mr. Buchanan."

"Well, if it's OK with your uncle, you can be my assistant today if you'd like."

"For sure!"

As I finished my chocolate milk and the men finished their coffee, Mr. Buchanan said, "Why don't I show you where the tools are so you'll know where to get them when I need them." I followed him over to the trunk of his car.

Placed on a blanket in the trunk was a beautiful wooden tool chest, which he opened at the top. A variety of hand saws were secured in the lid, each held in place with finished pieces of wood which turned on a center pin to allow the saws to be removed from their nesting places. The rest of the chest contained a series of drawers which could be pulled out by putting your finger into an indented brass ring. Each drawer contained a variety of tools in an orderly arrangement.

Mr. Buchanan pointed to the saws in the lid. "This is a cross-cut saw, this is a rip saw, and this is a miter saw. These other ones we won't be needing today. We'll use those when we are building cabinets. In this drawer are the plumb-bobs, and in this drawer are the rules, dividers, and compasses." Closing the lid of the toolbox, Mr. Buchanan turned a latch on each side and the top part separated from the bottom of the chest, revealing more tools, each held in place in its own built-in space. "This is where you can find the framing square and the smaller carpenter's squares."

I was overwhelmed with all the tools I'd never seen before along with a whole new vocabulary. Until that moment, I thought a carpenter only used a hammer and a saw. Little did I know that morning how much I was going to learn!

Mr. B handed me a yellow wooden folding rule and said, "Here you are, you'll be needing this. Know how to use it?" I said "Yes." Well after all, I had used a 12" wooden ruler in school and we had a tape measure at home. I knew how to read fractions of an inch. What else did I need to know? I did notice that on the first fold of this wooden rule there was a little metal piece that you could slide out and then push back in. Interesting, I thought... I wonder what that's for and how the heck do you fold and unfold this thing and why? I had so much to learn.

That Saturday was the first of many 'helping' Mr. Buchanan because after that day, I wanted to go to the construction site every weekend. Mr. Buchanan insisted I call him Bucky but even after many weeks, the best I could ever do was to call him Mr. B.

Mr. Buchanan insisted that everything must be 'plumb' and that was the purpose of the plumb-bob. He taught me how to use it as a vertical reference which he called the plumb line. Everything, he insisted, was calculated right from the plumb line. From this line, you then used a tool called the square to make additional measurements and to determine angles. It was at this point that my high school math courses finally started to make some practical sense. I was simply amazed when Mr. B would pick up the large steel square and start laying out cut marks for hand sawing the rafters for the roof. He used a big flat sided pencil to make the marks where cuts needed to be made for the rafters to fit together perfectly on the notches at the bottom and the angles at the top. Mr. Buchanan would calculate the slope of the roof for cutting the rafters with that same carpenter's square and a pencil. When he laid out the pencil marks on the hip rafters for the different angles to be cut on a single 2X6, I saw magic happen right before my eyes as each rafter fitted perfectly in place.

I can hear his voice even now. "Gary, what's the blueprint say regarding the slope? Is it 4/12, 5/12 or 6/12 pitch?" And I would say, "I can't tell." And he would say, "Well then, better bring the prints here so we can figure it out."

Now this wasn't a lot of fun for me since the prints were secured on a big sheet of plywood, covered with a piece of plastic. I soon learned that it was definitely to my advantage to figure out the answer to the question rather than lugging the prints on that awkward piece of plywood up to wherever Mr. B was working at the moment.

Finally, I was promoted from being a gofer to being able to use the hand saws. It was then that I learned how much work sawing was! After a full day of sawing floorboards, siding, studs, rafters, or joists, my arm ached pretty much all of Sunday and even into Monday and Tuesday. Mr. B taught me to 'read' the grain of the wood. There is a certain way to place floor joists and roof rafters based on the grain pattern. To cut a piece of wood across the grain, you had to use the crosscut saw. I can still hear his instructions. "Keep it lubed. Start the cut with the teeth nearest the handle for best control. Make a few back cuts until you develop a nice kerf."

He simply insisted on doing things right. "When you use the ripsaw, start the cut with the finer teeth furthest from the handle and near the point of the blade. Go slowly, make a few short draw strokes to develop the kerf. And whatever you do, do not cut right on the pencil or chalk line but cut right next to it on the waste side. And always measure everything twice before you cut anything."

My next promotion was to the hammer brigade. Mr. B instructed me: "This is a framing hammer, these are claw hammers — a 20 oz. and a 16 oz. Here are the finish hammers and the nail sets."

I thought a hammer was a hammer: how little I knew — after using that 20 oz. hammer to drive nails all day, it simply would not allow you to let it go. I actually had to pry my fingers open with my other hand to relax the 'muscle memory' and loosen my fingers to put it down at the end of the day. And I was so happy when we could go home 'early' because it was a Saturday and only 4 o'clock, as Mr. B reminded me each time as he began to pack up his tools.

On those Saturdays with Mr. Buchanan, I learned a new vocabulary, I learned to use tools properly and I learned a new work ethic. Since that eventful summer, I have built a year-round cabin, a garage and a building we call the Tea House, albeit with power tools and no hand saws. I have tried to live by the lessons Mr. B taught me all those years ago. Alas, I have failed to keep my vehicles clean and shiny like he did, even when he had to park at the dusty, muddy construction site. Oh, and one other thing: I also don't have a Cadillac...

Where's the Owner?

At the time, it seemed like a great idea for a weekend of fun... travel with another 'classic Ford' couple from NY to Vermont for a car show. Our plans were to return on Sunday and Tony and Judi agreed to make reservations for the four of us in Burlington, VT. I agreed to find a place to stay on Sunday evening, somewhere around the halfway point home.

I checked the map and found a small town in the Adirondacks in the right area but I could not find a motel. Finally, I noticed Pleasant Valley Ski Resort — it looked to be near the town and offered rooms. I called the number listed on the website and tried to make reservations for the four of us. Oddly, considering that it was summer and a ski lodge is not usually busy in the summer, the female taking the information was hesitant when I inquired if the resort had any vacancies. "Well let me check, I'll call you back." A half hour later, she called back. "When did you say you needed those rooms? I think we can accommodate you but you need to know it is off season. I inquired, "Is that a problem?" She responded, "No, but I won't be here if that's OK with you." I made the reservations without another thought.

The car show was exciting and we had a great time in Burlington. Sunday afternoon, we headed out and found our way to the ski lodge which turned out to be well off the main road. Right from the get-go, things seemed strange. First off, referring to this as a resort was a big stretch as the large parking lot lay in front of a small, old fashioned ski lodge. The building needed paint and repairs and the only vehicle in the lot was an old 1961 Caddy. Tony and I — the car guys — checked it out carefully. The paint was faded and the rear tire on the passenger's side was almost flat. It had been in that spot for a long, long time. From the parking lot, we could see a log fence in front of the lodge with big windows looking into what we thought was a dining room. Near the front entrance, there was a large pile of wood with a long-handled ax buried in a wood stump.

There was absolutely no sign of life.

After a long pause in front of the door, I said bravely, "Shall we go in?"

Opening the door to a hallway, we could see a large dining room to our left and at the end of the hall, a stairway leading upstairs with a closed door on the right. We looked around for a reception area, or a desk, or even a phone... but there was nothing.

"Hello, hello, anybody here?" There was no reply.

We slowly walked into the dining room. At first glance, all looked ready for dinner: there were white tablecloths on all the tables, three long buffets were stacked with serving dishes, table centerpieces, cups and saucers, plates, and candle holders — there were even candles. But the chandeliers all had cobwebs on them. I walked over to the nearest sideboard and noticed all the dishes had a layer of dust on them — one cup even had a spider's web on the handle.

"Hello, hello!" I called out again, louder this time. Again, no response.

Turning to the others huddled up behind me, I whispered, "Tony, Judi, this is really weird, don't you think?"

Suddenly there was a deep voice from the doorway behind us. "Hello there." We all jumped.

We turned and walking toward us was the perfect image of a 'mountain man' dressed in a flannel shirt and Levis, with tall, laced woodsman's boots. "I'm Jim... wasn't expecting to see you this early. Sorry I didn't hear you come in. I was on the phone with the owner of this place. She's not here now; she's in Florida and leaves me to run things while she's gone." He looked out the windows. "Mighty fine cars you got out there. What are they?"

Gary and Tony replied, in chorus: "Fords — a 1940 and a 1932."

Jim said: "Mind if I take a picture of them when I can find my camera?" And then, gesturing to our huddle in the doorway, he said, "Come on in."

We followed him down the hallway to the closed door at the end. It turned out to be a cozy room with a fire in the wood stove, a sofa and big, comfortable chairs covered with throws. There was a deer head on the wall and underneath, two deer legs bent at the ankles, attached to a wall plaque, holding a lever action rifle.

"How long you here for?" Jim asked.

"Just tonight. I made reservations."

"I knew you were coming." Jim said. "We're closed until the snow comes and the chair lift opens, usually in December. Like I said, the owner is in Florida for the off season and I take care of the place while she's gone. She told me you were coming so I went to town yesterday for supplies."

Looking out at the parking lot, Tony asked, "How far is it into town?"

Jim replied, "About eight miles, give or take."

Remembering the Caddy that clearly hadn't moved in years, I spoke up. "I see the car out front has a flat tire."

"Yeah, I've got to fix that. I hitched a ride into town. Let me show you your rooms."

Mountain man Jim led us out into the hall and up the stairs to the second floor where a hall extended from one side of the building to the other with doors on both sides.

Jim turned and said: "Is this OK? I have rooms on the third floor where it is quieter if you prefer them."

I'm thinking...quieter? It is clear that none of us are exactly thrilled at the situation. A general mumbling followed before Tony spoke up. "No, no. This floor is fine."

Jim led the four of us down the hall to room 8 and asked, "Who wants this room?"

I looked at my sweetie. Her eyes rolled, her shoulders shrugged, and I interpreted. "This is fine."

Jim proceeded on down the hall. "OK...let's get the other room for you guys..."

Off the four of us go again, past several more doors to room 12.

Turning to Judi and Tony, he said: "And here's your room."

And then he disappeared before we realized how far apart our rooms were. We just stood there, staring at each other. Finally, we all went together to the cars to pick up our bags.

"We didn't ask him about dinner." I said as we trudged across the parking lot. I noticed we were doing everything together, but I didn't say anything.

Just before we reached the front door, Judi turned suddenly and whispered: "I don't care what you guys think — this is too weird. We are all staying together until we go to bed."

I admit, I was wondering about the lady who owned the place. Where WAS she? The whole thing felt very strange. But we did need dinner so we went to Jim's door and knocked...

We heard, "Yes, just a minute." It seemed like an hour before the door opened.

As the designated speaker, I said, "What time is dinner tonight?"

Jim: "Dinner is at 7. When do you want breakfast tomorrow?"

"How about 7?" I asked. "And can we move our rooms next to each other?"

Jim replied. "Can't do that...remodeling. Those are the only two rooms we have."

And now we were all wondering, why had he offered us rooms on the third floor?

We climbed the stairs and went to our rooms together, dropping off our bags as a group.

Judi spoke up. "I wonder about the remodeling part? I'm going to see what's in these other rooms."

And again as a group, we exited to the hall to find all the doors locked.

"OK, this is just too weird." Judi spoke up again. "Should we even stay here tonight?"

I said: "I don't think we have too many choices. I think we stay. But I do wonder if the owner is REALLY in Florida. Do you think Mountain Man got rid of her and is taking over the place?"

Dinner at 7 was surprisingly nice although the cobwebs on the chandeliers were still there. The table was set with clean dishes and there were platters of cold cuts and baskets of bread. There was an urn of fresh coffee, and sodas to drink. Dessert was a warm, fresh cherry pie. Jim left us alone but he did come back to offer ice cream to go with the pie.

We stayed in the dining room for the rest of the evening and all headed up together to the second floor about ten. But as we went by the front door, we noticed the ax was gone, no longer wedged into the stump. My heart jumped and we all crushed together and raced up the stairs. At the top, we decided to prop chairs against the door handles since there were no interior locks on our doors and whispered goodnight.

It was a long, long night. About 11 we heard chopping out behind the building. From the windows, we could see a long shadow on the lawn — someone moving and chopping wood. Then for the next half hour, we heard the back door opening and the screen door slamming closed, over and over again. Who chops wood in the middle of the night, I thought and kept thinking... I hope that's wood he's chopping... why so many trips in and out?

Daylight could not come fast enough. I was dog tired and wide awake at 5:30am — amazing, as I was not a morning person. At 6:45, we walked down to room 12 and knocked. A small voice responded from the other side of the door, "Who's there?"

"Just us. Are you guys ready for breakfast?"

"YES!" They were sitting on the edge of the bed, already packed and ready to go. We were so happy to see each other we actually hugged!

No Jim to be seen as we entered the huge dining room but everything was set up for us. Breakfast was fine — toast, jams, dry cereal, milk, and coffee. Around 20 minutes later, Mountain Man showed up with a camera and asked if he could take a picture of us with our cars. We were on the road immediately thereafter.

* * * * * * * *

Looking back, I can't say why we were so freaked out. Things just didn't add up. Somehow, we were certain Jim had killed the owner and hidden her body. For several weeks after the trip, we anxiously watched the news to see if a woman from the Adirondacks was reported missing but eventually that worry faded. By the time ski season arrived, we had all but forgotten our terrifying overnight stay. I don't recommend it but if you do wish to stay at the Pleasant Valley Lodge, I still have the phone number.

I Don't Know if it Happened This Way . . .

The Secret Fishing Hole in Munsen

The dirt road we were driving on cut through a stunted growth of pines that lined both sides, blocking any sight into the woods for more than twenty feet. The only possible view in the distance was the road ahead which we'd been focused on for hours. Our gas tank was reading low, near the last quarter mark from empty. We had been told the town of Munsen had two gas pumps at the old country store but there had been no road signs to this point of the trip and I knew for sure we hadn't missed any turn-offs or junctions. When we left the main highway, the road was smooth and dusty but now it was just two dirt tracks with grass growing up in the middle, much less traveled than when we started out. We had stopped several times along the way, once to check the ropes on the old wooden boat on the roof rack, once to grab a beer and sandwich from the cooler and once to pee but we hadn't seen a single sign of life.

Jerry kept harping about running out of gas. I was also worried but I wasn't saying anything yet, just hoping this wasn't a wild goose chase. We'd been promised that we'd find the best fishing hole ever just outside of Munsen. The old guy we'd met at Duffy's Bar had told us about this secret spot. He said he had lived up in Munsen before the mine petered out and everyone left. He said Jameson's — the old general store — was still open and the three or four families still left in town depended on it. He told us where to turn off Highway 10A onto this dirt road but why we didn't check the route and our destination on a map before leaving town was completely beyond me right now. Coulda, woulda, shoulda...

The old beat-up Chevy wasn't giving us much confidence at that moment either. We'd talked about turning around and going back when the tank hit the half full mark but we hadn't wanted to give up on this adventure, this very special fishing trip. But by this time, Jerry was nervous and wanted to turn around and go back. I kept saying, "What would our buddies say if they saw us coming back into town without any fish?"

The old duffer had said it was the most amazing fishing spot he'd ever thrown a line into: "I'm telling you, this is the truth and it isn't just the beer talking; I swear on my wife's grave it's so!" We made plans for the three of us to leave the next Friday for the weekend, right after Jerry and I got out of work. As he promised, the old guy was at Duffy's but when we stopped by to pick him up, he backed out. He went on and on about his son coming to see him this weekend and how he had to stick around as he hadn't seen him since he left Munsen the month after graduation to join the Marines. Jerry was disgusted with this story and thought it was pure BS but I told him, "Cut him a little slack — we don't need him since we know where we're going anyway. And besides, we don't have enough beer to keep him happy."

We had gotten an early start, a little before 5:30 in the afternoon; not too bad, I thought at the time. We had driven without stopping for three hours and it was a little strange that we hadn't seen a car in either direction, or passed a house, or seen any sign of life in all that time. Jerry was asleep with his head bouncing off the back of the seat with every bump in the road like a little kid too tired to stay awake. The only thing I had seen for the last three hours was those pine trees. Suddenly, there was a break in the trees and I could see water.

"Looks like a river!" I said to Jerry as I poked him on the arm. He sat up straight, now wide awake. After a few more miles following the river's edge, we noticed a bridge ahead, a log bridge with planks nailed in place for the wheels to follow. We stopped the car to check it out before crossing: a few of the logs and planks were rotten and some were missing but I asked Jerry to guide me and I crept slowly across in first gear — the stop and go method — and we made it OK. On the other side, the road widened a bit and we pulled over.

It was getting late, the sun was setting and the soft sandy loam seemed like a good spot to pop up our tent for the night. Jerry was still bitching at me about running out of gas and not being able to get to Munsen and the general store to get more but we put our sleeping bags down in the tent and then grabbed our fishing poles, the flashlight, and a plastic container. In the woods, we found some old logs on the ground, turned them over and soon had a dozen or so grubs to use as bait. Sitting on the edge of the bridge we cast out, and bingo, we each caught a big one. Nearly every time we threw out a line, we had a hit and pulled in a beautiful fat pike or walleye. Jerry was now all smiles, "Looks like we're gonna have a fantastic dinner tonight!"

Soon a roaring fire was set and the filleted fish were frying in butter in the cast iron frying pan. A few beers to wash the fish down and sleep came quickly. In the middle of the night, we were startled awake by a rubbing sound on the side of the tent. We were both scared stiff — we sat there without moving a muscle for what seemed like an hour. Eventually, it became quiet again and we both fell back to sleep. In the morning, I noticed moose tracks around the tent and called Jerry over,

"Must be a moose was licking the dew off the tent during the night — what the heck were you so scared about?"

We had a big breakfast and then decided we no longer needed to go to Munsen as this was the best fishing spot we had ever encountered. "There couldn't be anything better than this! Maybe this is the spot the old guy was telling us about but he forgot it was by the bridge before you got to town."

But for both of us, even at this moment of exultation, the gas problem still existed and if we ever hoped to get home for work on Monday we needed to make some decisions. Jerry suggested, "I got this figured out, it's simple. We'll just stay here, fish our brains out and catch a ride with the next car or truck passing by."

Even though we hadn't actually seen a car since we turned off the highway, I agreed, "Yeah, great plan! Just to make sure we don't miss an opportunity for a ride, I'll pull the car over to block the bridge in case we're asleep when someone comes along."

The fishing was fantastic. Days passed by as we waited for that good Samaritan to come by on the road to Munsen. But not a single car or truck ever appeared and finally, we had eaten every single thing in the cooler we had packed for the trip.

Jerry started in again, "We can't continue to stay here. We need a ride or we need gas or we need to head back and see how far we can get." I hated to admit it but he was right. The very next morning we packed everything up and crept back across the bridge for the last time. Suddenly, Jerry shouted, "Stop! We have the boat, stupid! Why don't we take it to the river and go down stream and see where we come out?" I just stared at him, "Are you crazy, we could be in that boat for days and who knows where we'd end up? We have no idea where this river goes."

After much deliberation, the discussion turned bitter when neither of us could convince the other we were right and we decided to part company. I was determined to stay with the car and make it as close to home as possible, walking the rest of the way when I ran out of gas if need be. Jerry thought I was crazy so I helped him unload the boat and put it in the river, and then we said goodbye. Neither one of us had any food but one of the fishing poles went with Jerry in the boat. I stood on the bridge watching for a long time as the boat drifted down river with the current, waving goodbye the whole time. Finally, Jerry and the boat disappeared around a bend in the river and I stood in silence, listening to my heart beating in my chest and feeling very much alone.

Slowly, I walked to the car, slid in behind the steering wheel and drove back down the road towards home, trying to get the best possible gas mileage, shutting off the engine every time I could coast down even the slightest grade. I drove until dusk and then fell asleep very hungry, stretched out as best I could on the back seat. The sky lightened a bit around 5:30 but I finally woke up when my watch showed 7:04, stiff and sore. I got out of the car, stretched my legs, slid back in behind the wheel and set off again. The inevitable happened at 4:42 in the afternoon. First a few skips and jerks and then the engine quit. The needle was way below the E mark on the instrument panel gauge. No doubt about it, I was out of gas.

Night came too quickly and I crawled into the back seat again. It seemed like morning would never come. Then, suddenly, it was bright and I was so hungry. Another day and night passed before I decided to head out walking. After what seemed like 10 miles, I saw clouds of dust boiling up into the sky ahead of me. Was I dreaming? No — it was a pickup truck! I stood in the middle of the road waving my arms and the truck pulled up and stopped. I told the three guys in the cab I was out of gas and asked if they had any to spare. They told me they had just enough for their own trip — they were headed to Munsen to pick up an old hit 'n miss engine that had been abandoned when the mine closed. They told me Munsen was a ghost town. They were there last hunting season, stayed in the abandoned old store at night, and there was not a soul left there now. That's when they had spotted the old engine and wanted it for their collection. I asked if they knew the bridge was in bad shape and they showed me the truck bed full of lumber they were going to use to fix it so they could get across without going in the river.

I asked them if they knew where the river went. They told me it flowed north out past Munsen into the wilderness for many miles before joining another larger river that eventually flowed up into Hudson Bay. I begged them to take me with them -- I could help them fix the bridge, I could load the engine — but they said, "No room really, but thanks!" They promised they would pick me up on the way back the very next day. They were just going to pick up the engine and then head right back as they needed to be home on Sunday. It was then that I realized for the first time with a horrible sinking feeling that a whole week had passed since we left home. They gave me a pizza box with two slices left in it and a cold beer. I asked them how far it was to town from where we were and they said about 50 miles or so. Then they told me to sit tight, not to worry, and they would pick me up tomorrow by noon, no later.

Two days passed. The guys never came back. On day three, I started walking towards town, looking for water and berries along the road. I kept thinking of Jerry — he had all the water in the world to drink while I thought I was going to die of thirst right there on that godforsaken road in the pines...

I Don't Know if it Happened This Way . . .

/

Johnny

There was a steady buzz but no particular voice could be distinguished above the murmur of the room as the guys walked into Bob's Diner on the east side of Main Street, down near the railroad tracks. The men were meeting for their regular Saturday breakfast as they had for over 30 years. The gatherings began when they were all working together at the old Delco plant, long before they were forced to retire early when General Motors closed down production and sold the facility.

The guys usually paid attention to Johnny — he had the charismatic style of an old Italian neighborhood "boss" and everyone believed he knew all the angles, shortcuts, and deals. Not only was he mailed a disability check every month from GM, he also received a Social Security check from the Feds. His combined income was significantly greater than what the other guys were receiving, even those who had worked at the plant until the day it closed. It appeared that Johnny had beaten the system as he collected disability for 15 years while his buddies continued to sweat it out at Delco. His disability was based on a questionable work-related injury which just so happened to have been approved by his own doctor; even though it had been challenged by Delco's medical doctor; the case was ultimately decided by the workman's compensation board in Johnny's favor.

In addition to his retirement benefits, Johnny had a number of other money-making operations. For many years, he ran an illegal high-stakes poker game at one of his rental properties late at night. During the day, he operated an unlicensed body shop in the two-car garage located on the same property. In addition, he provided a food service over the back fence at the Delco plant where he used to work. He made sandwiches in the afternoon in the basement of the house, supplying dinner to the guys working the evening shift. Orders were taken from the third shift workers for their scheduled dinner break and Johnny would prepare the sandwiches and deliver them at the appointed time. In addition to the price of the sandwich, there was a one-dollar service charge paid to the person inside the plant who took the orders and collected the preset charge — all of which was turned over to Johnny before he made up the bagged lunches. Everyone knew fifty cents of the service charge found its way right back into his pocket — another great income stream for Johnny. To all his buddies and everyone else in the plant, it seemed clear that Johnny was making more in retirement than anyone still working, even when every penny of overtime pay was included.

With all this action, Johnny was pretty busy, running his poker games, the body shop, and his sandwich business while the other retired guys were enjoying the seasons wintering in Florida, fishing in the summer and hunting in the fall. Any leftover free time was consumed with trips to the casinos to play the slots and to the track to bet on the ponies and enjoy a few beers. Johnny, on the other hand, was always thinking about new ways to expand his business empire. All this money did mean he also worried about his own personal safety since he always carried hundreds of dollars on his person. To ensure his own safety, he carried a .38 snub nose revolver in the back right hand pocket of his pants, next to his handkerchief. He never hesitated to pull it out when a card game got out of control, when there was a disagreement on a body shop bill, or when he went to collect money owed to the "bank" for a loan made at one of his poker games. He was always good for a loan to a loser who wanted to continue to play and try to recoup the money he had lost.

On this particular Saturday breakfast meeting over coffee, toast, eggs, sausage, and home fries, the usual conversation took a new twist:

"Hey Johnny, I see you closed early this morning. I came around midnight for a few hands but no one was there."

"Tell me about it..."

"No shit. No cars on the street, no lights on, your place was closed up tighter than a drumhead."

"Yeah, the cops shut me down around 10."

"What's the matter Johnny boy, no longer tight with the cops?"

"Shut your trap, you know I don't kiss ass."

"So what's the deal?"

"No deal, I'm open tonight. Tell the boys, big game tonight, big pots."

The following Saturday, the guys met as usual at the diner.

"Geez Johnny, sorry to hear about the fire. Read it in the paper and saw the film on the TV news Friday."

"Yeah, lost the house, garage, and the T-bird. Can you believe it, the day before the fire, a guy stops in with this '56 Thunderbird and wants a complete high dollar restoration paint job. So, I shoot him a good price and he leaves the car and a $5K deposit. Then the garage and the Bird burn to the ground and the fire spreads to the back porch and kitchen and burns that place to the ground too."

"Boy, he must be sick about his T-bird — and pissed off."

"Naw. I called him up and told him to report the loss to my insurance company and he'd be covered."

"Did he ask for his deposit back?"

"I told him if he split the insurance check with me, I'd find a better car in California for him, paint it for free and kick in an extra $5K along with his deposit. He has a written estimate that his '56 was worth 30 grand and he only has 8 grand into it plus the deposit he gave me so we'll both make out OK."

"What about the poker game?"

"I'm moving the games to my other rental on Rohr Street. The hell with the cops. It'll take them months to figure out where the game moved to, so spread the word, big game, big bucks, easy pickings at 179 Rohr Street Saturday, usual starting time."

"Hey Johnny, how much insurance did you have on the Plymouth Ave place?"

"Counting garage equipment, tools, house and contents, totals out to $250K and I have receipts and photos for everything that was in the place. All the good shit is now in my garage on Rohr St and I'm open for business right now. Boys, when the checks start coming in and I'm made whole, I promise all of you, I'm buying breakfast for everyone. I don't forget my friends and each of you is one of my best friends."

* * * * * * * *

Postscript. Eleven months later the following appeared in the B section of the local newspaper...

John M. Pasinatti of 179 Rohr St., age 67, found guilty of arson and sentenced to 7-13 years including current time served while awaiting conviction. Mr. Pasinatti was found guilty of setting a fire which destroyed a house and garage at 1225 Plymouth Ave in the city. He was also fined for failing to remove hazardous materials and the dangerous remains of two structures on the property. Additionally, he has been ordered to pay the city the amount of $13,287.67 for labor by city work crews to complete the removal of said materials and the remaining structures plus filling and leveling of the lot. Additionally, he is fined $5,045.75 for taxes owed.

Mother Ann Meets Long John Silver

What does a wooden box of Gorton's Mother Ann Codfish and a 78 RPM record of Treasure Island have to do with this story? This is how it all unfolded...

In 1950, I was 10 years old. Grandma worked all week at the Evening in Paris perfume factory in Rochester and Gramps was employed as a machinist in a local shop. Saturday was their big day off: Grandma always went shopping and I could go with her or stay home with Gramps. There was a downside to staying home even though I was allowed to spend my time playing with friends in the neighborhood. It was a given that I would have lunch with Gramps: I could go out and play all morning, but I had to be home at noon to eat.

Grandpa's Saturday routine featured fried codfish cakes for lunch — his favorite meal of the week. Around 10 o'clock he would take a wooden box of Gorton's Mother Ann Dried and Salted Codfish out of the cupboard and open it by sliding off the beveled cover. He broke the cod into flakes and dropped them into a pan of water to soak. Just before the clock chimed noon, he took the wet cod in his hands, squeezed out all the water, and placed it in a bowl. Next, he added diced leeks and pepper — no salt was needed! — and then mixed it all together to make codfish patties. Into the cast iron skillet sizzling and sputtering with butter went the patties. Fried to a golden brown on both sides, a huge platter of patties was placed on the table and we were ready for lunch. As good as they looked, I always covered the one patty I had to eat with a mountain of ketchup: Heinz was my friend and savior for those Saturday lunches!

After lunch, I was always given the empty wooden box, still redolent of fish.

That same year, one of my Christmas presents was a Peter Pan Treasure Island record which I played over and over. On the back sleeve was a picture of a treasure map, the chart for Treasure Island. In a flash, the idea struck me like a lightning bolt from the sky: buried treasure and a map to find it! This needed careful planning...

I searched the house and found the perfect paper for the map, a brown paper bag from Hart's Grocery Store. Let's see — I also needed scissors, colored pencils, India ink, a pen and matches. Matches were going to be a problem as I was forbidden to carry them. Or play with them. But the map was going to be the best treasure map ever found — somehow, I would have to find matches. But the first order of business was the treasure! Combing through every drawer in the house yielded a perfect haul: a handful of change, a broken watch, two unmatched earrings, a silver dollar, several war uniform metals, a pocket knife, and Indian head pennies. All these treasures fit nicely into the codfish box.

I carefully drew a map with "X marks the spot." Dotted lines were drawn from the pond down the street to the X. But the map still looked like it was drawn on a brown paper bag. I knew I could fix that! While Gramps was out working in the garden, I snuck down to the cellar where the box of wooden matches was kept by the coal furnace. Taking five matches from the box, I headed to the garage with my map. I used all five to burn the edges of the map, carefully blowing out the flames as each match burned down. At one point, I had to drop the map and stomp on it to put out a small fire but that actually improved the final aging process.

A little oil from the garage oil can rubbed on the map completed the masterpiece.

Now to find the perfect place to bury the treasure. I took the garden shovel out of the garage, went to the bank behind the grape vines and planted the box deep. I raked old grass, leaves, and trimmed-off vines over the area. The treasure was hidden! The rest of the afternoon was spent talking to all the guys in the neighborhood about treasure maps and planting rumors of buried treasure.

Amazingly, Johnny who lived across the street found an old treasure map on Tuesday after school when he spotted it under a rock, near the telephone pole by his mailbox. Word of his unbelievable find spread like wildfire: everyone crowded around to see the map! We made a pact to keep the map secret until Saturday morning when we could all go together to the pond and follow the route to the treasure.

Saturday arrived. The map had clues and was pretty easy to follow until we got to my house when the boys started wondering why the treasure was buried in my back yard. "I don't know — it's just the way it is..." I answered. "Come on... let's follow the map."

This proved easier said than done. Most of the guys just wanted to give up and go for a bike ride but I was a great cheerleader and kept them enthused and on task. Finally, Johnny hit pay dirt: excitement abounded when the little wooden box appeared! Johnny demanded that he keep the silver dollar and the rest of the spoils were divided among the other treasure hunters. I asked for the silver dollar but there was no way was Johnny going to relinquish it. I even begged, but it didn't matter. I was the loser even if the treasure had been found in my yard. Johnny was bigger than I was, and that was the end of that!

Weeks passed. One Saturday, Grandpa asked if I happened to know what happened to the silver dollar he had in the cuff link box in his shirt drawer. Somehow, I found my codfish cake needed ketchup at that very moment. I still love Heinz ketchup on a codfish cake but I'm not sure Mother Ann would have agreed with me, and for sure, I know Gramps never would! As for the missing silver dollar, it seems it was misplaced forever and Gramps never asked me about it again.

Foxhole Radio

The old Greek Revival styled farmhouse sat empty and what was formally a beautiful lawn was now a hay field. The family that had most recently lived there had moved out and planned to dismantle the house and salvage the lumber to build a new home on the same property. Before demolition started, there was an irresistible opportunity for Harold and Burgess to explore the place undetected; all they had to do was be silent and invisible.

It was a beautiful summer day and the early morning wind blew the tall grass in the front yard like waves in the ocean. Somewhere on the other side of the house, one of the green wooden shutters banged on the clapboards in sync with the waves in the hay. Burgess was fourteen and knew the family that had lived there — before they had moved out, he had attended the one-room school house just across the road with several of the children. Harold was eight and had only ever attended the centralized school after reorganization so he didn't know anyone in the family.

"Burgess, I don't think we should be here. What if somebody driving by sees us?"

"Harold, stop being a chicken. Last night at the camp-out you were scared out of your wits by the screech owl we heard in the middle of the night when the coy dogs were howling. You're just a baby. I told you not to be afraid of them and now I'm telling you the same thing."

Harold subsided and the boys ran around to the back of the house and then carefully made their way to the side porch and the kitchen door. It was unlocked and they tiptoed into the kitchen and then through the pantry into the living room and dining room. Down the hall, they looked into both bedrooms. The door to the upstairs was closed. The place was empty, airless and completely still.

Breathlessly, Harold whispered, "Burgess, that's enough, let's get out of here."

"Not so fast chickenshit, let's see what's upstairs."

Burgess turned the doorknob and slowly opened the door. He held the knob in his hand for a moment, feeling the multiple edges and noticing the reflection of light in the depth of the diamond shapes in the glass. Glancing up, the boys saw there was a closed door to a room at the top of the stairs but the doors to two other rooms were wide open. Although they tried to be quiet, it was impossible as each step creaked loudly. At the top of the landing, they saw that the bedroom on the right was empty but in the larger bedroom on the left, there was a closet with a closed door. They tiptoed over and opened it but it was also completely empty. What a disappointment this whole expedition was turning out to be!

"Burgess, I'm going."

"Harold, wait a minute, we only have one more room to explore, then we can go."

Back on the landing. Burgess turned the doorknob to the last room, once again admiring the cut-crystal diamond glass knob, cool in this palm. He turned it and pushed on the door, but something was keeping it from opening. He pushed a bit harder — the knob rattled a bit but then the door shifted open a few inches allowing the boys to peek in. They saw piles of old radios, radio cabinets, boxes of tubes, old television sets with small round screens, and radio and television parts and tubes everywhere. The floor was completely covered in radios and TVs and piles of parts. Burgess pushed his way in, forcing the door open and in the process, radios and boxes of parts on the floor gave way as they slid and piled into each other. Tubes cascaded to the floor with a series of loud crashes.

"Burgess, come on, we got to go, you're breaking stuff. We're going to get caught."

Burgess just pulled on the strap of Harold's bib overalls, yanking him into the room and then, leaning back against the door, forced it closed. He started picking up tubes, throwing them against the white plaster walls and breaking the glass tubes.

Harold cried out, "Burgess, stop!" But then something on the floor caught his eye. "Look at this!"

He had picked up a set of old Army headphones attached to a small board holding a spool of wire wrapped around an empty cardboard tube; a double-edged razor blade was stuck into the board and another wire was attached to a safety pin.

"Burgess, what do you think this is?"

"God, Harold, you don't know nothing... it's a foxhole radio."

"What's it for? What does it do?"

Squatting down beside Harold with the apparatus in his hand, Burgess said, "Harold, I told you already... my dad was in the Army with the guy who used to live here and I heard them talk about these things a lot — how they built them, how they used them, how they'd listen to them at night during the war. It was like a crystal radio only it didn't need no electricity or battery. It was entertainment for them. They just wanted to listen to jazz, dance music — any news they could get. The Jerries and the Japs used their radio broadcasts as propaganda."

"How do you make it work?"

"Simple, dummy. You moved the point of the pin slowly across the razor blade until you found a radio station and then you just listened through the headphones."

"Burgess, set it up. Let me try it..."

Burgess helped Harold put the headset on, then handed him the board and told him to move the pin slowly and carefully over the razor blade. When he heard something, he should stop on that spot. Harold did as he was told and after a moment or two, his eyes grew as big as saucers. Through his head set he heard...

"Hello Suckers! Well kids, you know I'd like to say to you, 'Pack up Your Troubles in Your Old Kit Bag,' but I know that little old kit bag is much too small to haul all the troubles you kids have got. The wonderful boys of the 504th Parachute Regiment — Col. Willis Michell's playboys in the 61st Troop Carrier Group are going to carry you to certain death. We know where and when you are jumping and you will be wiped out. "Between the Devil and the Deep Blue Sea, a sweet kiss from Sally Zucca." *

Harold was terrified. He grabbed the headset off, handed the board to Burgess, and fled, flying down the stairs. Burgess could hear him shouting just before the back door slammed. "I'm going to tell my parents about this!"

Alone, Burgess tripped over a radio set on the floor and fell back against the door which slammed shut behind him. He put on the headset and moving the pin slowly across the razor blade he heard...

"Greetings everybody! This is your little playmate — I mean your bitter enemy — Ann, with a program of dangerous and wicked propaganda for my victims in Australia and the South Pacific. Stand by, you unlucky creatures, here I go! So be on your guard and mind the children don't hear! All set? Okay! Here's the first blow at your morale — the Boston Pops playing, 'Strike Up the Band!' My favorite family of boneheads, the fighting G.I.s in the blue Pacific..." *

Burgess dropped the board, turned and grabbed the doorknob but the door seemed to be stuck closed. He pulled harder, rattling the door, and suddenly the knob came off in his hand. No longer did he notice the coolness of the glass nor its beautiful diamond shape reflecting light. He stood silent, looking down at his hand and all he felt was a darkness he had never experienced before. The only sound he could hear now was the pounding of his heart, ready to burst from his chest...

*These transmissions are verbatim from the radio recordings made during WWII by both the US Army and Navy.

The Bet

Winslow was wise beyond his years but his parents couldn't have known that when they encumbered him with a 300-year-old formal family name for the rest of his life. Fortunately, Winslow turned out to be a genuinely gifted child and a real piece of work — his name didn't begin to do justice to his abilities or his imagination. He won the school's spelling bee when he was in 4th, 5th, and 6th grade and was champ in the state-wide spelling bee in 7th grade. By 8th grade, he'd been abducted by aliens and transported to Vulcan and returned to tell about it.

It all happened on the 4th of July according to Winslow. He convinced all the kids in the neighborhood that he had been abducted under cover of the town's fireworks show — he even had a bag of gold rocks to prove it. He showed all the girls the gem rocks and the marks on his arms where the Vulcans had hooked up electrodes to transfer the knowledge of the intellectuals of their planet directly to his brain. "Just watch me in high school next year," he told them, "I'll never have to study and I'll make all the honor rolls. Bet you I can!" The girls smiled and whispered and then walked away. They liked Winslow — he was smart and cute, even if he was a bit odd.

Well, Winslow's predictions proved to be valid and really, no one was surprised. But trouble was brewing in his senior year. Girls liked him. He was helpful, kind and sweet, treating them all with respect. But he wasn't well liked by the guys at all. They admired him at a distance for his scholarly achievements and his personality, but he was so easy to pick on.

On April 1st, the guys cornered him in the locker room and asked him who he was taking to the Senior Prom.

They told him, "You have the wisdom of every Vulcan from their planet; you can ask anyone you want. Remember that stunt you pulled on us in 7th grade? You should have no trouble asking Hillary to the Prom."

Winslow had never had a date with any girl in the school as far as the guys knew, much less the head cheerleader. But Winslow bragged that he would have no trouble getting Hillary to go to the prom with him. Jeffery, the captain of the football team, got in his face and shouted, "Oh yeah, I'll bet you twenty-five dollars — no way in hell she'll go with you."

Winslow replied, "That's chump change — you've got to make it worthwhile for me to use my Vulcan powers." He turned to face the group. "I'll tell you what. You get me 50 guys to bet twenty-five dollars each, put it in writing and have the money up front, and I will do it. And just so you know I'm serious, I'll put up the registration to my Buick to hold along with your bet money to make this transaction legitimate and binding and worth my time."

The guys couldn't believe their luck: they would end up with Winslow's Buick which was worth at least $3,000, just for putting up $25 each on this bet. How could they lose? Hillary was never going to go to the prom with this guy and everyone in the school knew it.

But Winslow had a plan. By Friday, word was all around school, 50 guys had their money in hand and the money and registration was given to Kenny to hold. Everyone knew Kenny; he had graduated the year before and worked at the family restaurant in town. Most of the kids went there after school to hang out and have an ice cream. Kenny was honest, trusted, and respected by all.

What the guys didn't know was that Winslow had called Hillary and asked if he could come over to talk to her and her mom and dad together about something special. Intrigued, she had agreed.

Four weeks later, prom night arrived. A big limo pulled up in front of the school and Winslow and Hillary walked in together, along with four other couples — Hillary's best friends and their dates. A hush fell, followed by an immediate buzz from the crowd.

"He pulled it off."

"The SOB, how'd he do that?"

"What the...?"

Seems Hillary and her mom and dad like honesty and someone who is smart, upfront, has a plan and likes a good joke — and donates $1,250 dollars to their daughter's college fund.

I Quit

At the time, it seemed like a good decision. With the new school year closing in fast, decisions had to be made. But what seemed like a good choice at the time proved to be disastrous.

As the saying goes, 'timing is everything.' I had just been hired as the new superintendent in a school district — my first posting as superintendent. I knew a lot was riding on my decisions, my job performance and leadership in terms of improving student outcomes. I was new to the community and the school district when I arrived in July to begin my tenure. During the first week, I suddenly realized that staffing for opening the school district in September was incomplete. Positions had to be advertised to attract and recruit candidates before hiring could even begin, but nothing had been done to even begin the process.

This particular school district was located in a rural community. Given this fact and that it was late in the summer, just before the school year was about to begin, trying to entice candidates to apply would be challenging because most career-oriented folks had started their job search months before and had already been hired. It was also a 'sellers' market' that year as there were plenty of openings across the state, many in wealthier and larger districts. Most recent college graduates sought job opportunities in the larger suburban districts: remote rural districts lacked interest for several pretty valid reasons including lower starting salaries; limited housing availability; no community of young professionals for interaction; minimal social opportunities; and distance from their home community and their own family members. So... hiring in a remote rural district was a challenge, to say the least. Nonetheless, by mid-August the district had received applications from advertisements placed in local and regional newspapers and the selection process was set to begin. In this particular small district, I was really the only one available to manage the hiring process including the final interviews. I was keenly aware how the person I hired would reflect on my judgment — good or bad.

One of the positions to be filled was that of high school English teacher and the district had received four applications. Background checks and phone conversations had eliminated two of the candidates, leaving two finalists. With the late start and all our limitations, I felt lucky to be interviewing Elizabeth Darcy. She was from Long Island, had graduated from a well-known university majoring in literature and theater, and had earned an excellent GPA. Her interview went very well — she was knowledgeable about pedagogy, confident, engaging and poised. I thought she was the best candidate for the students and the district, and I recommended to the board of education that she be hired.

Alas, I had not figured on the insecurity of this young, attractive female when faced with a difficult class of rowdy young men. In this rural farming and logging community, male students were known to be rude and obnoxious, especially to new teachers. Right from the outset, it was apparent that discipline was not Elizabeth's strong suit. With support from the principal and me, discipline in her classes gradually began to fall within almost acceptable bounds. Teaching and learning began to take place after the strategic transfer of a few of her most difficult students to another section with a male staff member who — although not really pleased with this administrative decision — understood the need. The entire staff was generally supportive of Elizabeth as a first-year teacher and much advice was shared in the faculty room. But the Christmas break could not come soon enough for Elizabeth who was more than pleased to leave her classes behind and return to Long Island with her family and friends.

New resolve for better discipline accompanied Elizabeth on her return to school in January and classroom management was marginally acceptable until almost the year-end review, just before final exams were to be given. One day in June, the high school principal called me and said Elizabeth had disappeared. It was reported that she walked out of her classroom after the lunch period, just as classes were getting underway. A quick investigation revealed the boys had been even more relentless than usual in disrupting instruction, absolutely refusing to engage in reviewing old Regents English exams. The girls said Elizabeth just closed the exam folder, said something about "an impossible situation" and "uncouth young men," and left the room. I glanced out the window towards the faculty parking lot and noticed her car was missing. The principal stayed with the class and I left.

I drove over to the general store where faculty and students shopped and asked Larry, the manager, if he had seen Miss Darcy today. He told me she had been there a short time ago and bought a six pack. He thought it was a bit strange that she stopped in so early in the afternoon, but then he thought perhaps school was out early for the day. He told me he didn't question her about why she was out so early but he did ask her where she was off to.

"Well Larry...what did she tell you?"

"Said she was going down to the river."

The river flowed through the center of town and at the bridge on the main highway, there was a turn-off leading to a park with a sandy beach and lifeguard stand. I drove the short distance to the park and there was Elizabeth's car. I glanced over towards the beach and sitting on a blanket spread on a large boulder was Elizabeth, with a beer in her hand and the opened six-pack lying at her feet in the sand. I parked and walked towards her.

"Hi, Liz."

"Hello, Mr. Buehler."

"Having a bad day?"

"You can say that again. I know I'm fired. I just can't teach those... those... blankety, blankety, overgrown little boys."

"I hear you. We're OK here right now at this moment. What you need to do is follow me back to school. Give me your beer and I'll pick up the rest. You just walk over, get in your car and follow me to the back parking lot."

Liz was compliant and we arrived at the back lot and proceeded directly to my office. We spent the next half hour talking through the situation. I listened patiently as she wound herself down a bit. The essence of the conversation unfolded as follows.

"I know you are going to fire me but that's OK. I don't care. I'm not coming back. I am never going to face those jerky little boys again."

"I understand how you feel but I don't think you really want to just walk out. I would have to fire you. It would be on your record and you might never be able to secure another teaching position if you are fired. Do you really want to give up teaching forever?"

"Not really. I would like to teach somewhere on Long Island, closer to home. I really want to get my master's degree and teach at the college level and not have to worry so much about discipline."

"If that is what you really want, then I suggest you take some time right now and write a letter of resignation. The less detail in your letter, the better. There is a major difference between being fired or resigning a position and I want to keep your options open. All the district needs is a letter of resignation. When you finish putting your thoughts down on paper, just leave the letter with me."

Elizabeth returned with her letter and we talked some more. This difficult year helped her to realize that she did love teaching English literature and really wanted to pursue a master's degree. At the next board meeting, I recommended to the members that we accept her letter of resignation, effective June 30th of that year. In the few weeks remaining until that date, she would be assigned the task of curriculum development for English. A substitute teacher would be assigned to her classes for the remaining days of instruction and administration and supervision of the final exams.

I learned a lot from Elizabeth — I learned that all the training in the world doesn't necessarily prepare you for the task at hand. Finding that out was a critical part of the hiring process and I carried that knowledge with me to four more postings as superintendent over the many years of my career. And I hope that somewhere out there is an educator with a master's degree, engaging young people in college or graduate school in learning English literature. Maybe she's even directing the school's play. Or at least, I like to think so...

Wondering

"Don't ever go in his yard, near his barn or house, or stop and visit with him." My aunt was very clear. I didn't understand why she was telling me this about Marty — after all, he came to my Aunt and Uncle's farmhouse every day. Marty was different — tall, lanky and unshaven, he always had a hand-rolled Red Man tobacco cigarette dangling from the corner of his mouth. A musty dank smell permeated Marty's clothes but when you were near him, he smelled of wood smoke, horse liniment, and sweat. For a 10- year-old, Marty was a different, curious older person — the most different and curious person I had ever met.

In the summers, I stayed with my aunt and uncle on their farm and I saw Marty every day. I would walk out past my uncle's barn and down the curved driveway to the hard-top road, turn right and go a bit further, right past Marty's place. His shack sat deep in a grove of tall pine trees. He had a horse shed close to the back door, which you couldn't see from the road. If Marty was sitting in the front room behind the four windows, he'd wave to me from his rocking chair and I'd wave back. Once I saw Marty plowing his garden with his horse Nelly and he stopped and waved to me. I walked down from the road to say hello and Marty carefully explained what he was doing and then sent me on my way. I liked Marty and I liked Nelly.

Marty had a routine that never varied. Like clockwork, he would appear at the kitchen door at 9 o'clock every morning with a large stainless pail in his hand. He'd knock, open the door and walk in, never waiting for anyone to let him in — he'd just come in and fill the pail with water at the sink. The pail was just like the ones Uncle George used in the dairy barn for milking the cows. Apparently, Marty's hand-dug well had gone dry that summer and thus the necessity for his daily walk to the farm with the bucket. When I asked about the pail, my aunt said my Uncle George had loaned it to him. Often, references were made to Marty when he wasn't around. Aunt Erma had commented to me that Marty was like Uncle George — they had both experienced tough times during the war and those experiences still affected them in various ways.

Marty had no social graces — no-one said anything, but I thought maybe this was a way the war had affected him. For sure, no words like "sorry" or "excuse me" ever emerged. There was just a single-minded focus on the task at hand — filling the pail with water and leaving for home. Not waiting for someone to answer the door before coming in led to embarrassing situations a few times — never embarrassing for Marty, but definitely for others. Once, the knock on the door occurred in the middle of someone taking a sponge bath at the kitchen sink. That time, the door opening was followed by a female's blood-curdling scream. For a 10-year-old lad, the finer points of these interactions were not understood but noticed.

One day, Marty didn't appear at the kitchen door as usual. At dinner, I heard my aunt say that Marty had been found on the path in front of his place, sprawled face-down on the ground with the bucket nearby. The sad, unspoken understanding was that Marty wouldn't be arriving anymore for water. I wondered what had happened.

The next morning, I walked out past the barn, down towards Marty's place and stood on the side of the road, trying to see if there was a spot in the tall grass where he had fallen. There were no clues. The magnetic draw was too great for me so I slipped down the path past the shack to the horse shed. Slowly, I opened the large door and peaked in. Nelly was gone. Her leather harness still hung on the wall, but Nelly was gone. Poor Nelly, I thought — first Marty is gone and now Nelly. I loved that horse because Marty loved her and they worked so well together. I wondered what had happened to Nelly.

As I backed out of the shed and pushed the door closed, I turned and saw Marty's ax was still buried in the wood-splitting stump near the wood pile by the back door. I tried to pull the ax out, but it didn't budge. I stood looking at the back door of Marty's home. The window to the right of the door had bottles lined up on the sill covering all the lower panes of glass. I tried the knob and the door opened! Inside, I looked carefully at the windowsill. A green Mason jar with a glass lid on it sat, empty. Other bottles of various shapes and colors attracted my attention. All were covered with dust and cobwebs. As I took each one down to examine it, I wondered what Marty had used them for. One was labeled Andrew's Liver Salts, another, Carter's Liver Pills; there was a bottle of Doan's Pills and Loran's Indian Oil, and larger bottles with labels of Old Crow, Fireball, and Seagram's. All were completely dry.

The sink under the window was also empty. The small wood cookstove next to the window had a pot on it with dried beans in it. The waste barrel next to the stove was filled to the brim with empty tin cans, all with their jagged tops still attached. To my left was the entrance to a tiny bedroom with a single white iron bed and a stand with an oil lamp on it. Funny, I thought, there is no door to the bedroom. I looked around: no radio, no refrigerator, no toaster. Then it dawned on me — no electricity. On the other wall was a wooden cabinet, almost empty except for a can of Maxwell House coffee with a few teaspoons left in it, two cans of sardines in mustard sauce, and a can of Campbell's pork and beans.

Another doorway also missing a door led out to the small front room with four windows across the front. There was Marty's rocking chair beside a wicker stand with an oil lamp on it. This is where Marty waved to me as I rode my wagon down the hill from the barn. Back in the kitchen, I noticed a wooden bench piled high with magazines, all covered with a thick layer of dust. All were Life magazines, in chronological order by year, with the oldest on the bottom. The top one was dated September, 1945. Many of the covers were photos of WWII... I remembered my aunt telling me about how Uncle George and Marty had been in the big war and how their memories still bothered them. I began looking through the Life magazines, one by one. I saw things I had never seen before — terrible pictures of the battles of the war. I began to understand just a little bit why Marty didn't have much to say when he came for water and how strangely he acted, just knocking and walking right in. For some reason, I thought again about the pail he used and how it was exactly like the ones Uncle George used in the barn.

As I left, I shut the back door. I tried pulling the ax out of the stump once more but still no luck. I was going back to Aunt Erma's with nothing to remind me of Marty. I walked up the path wondering just where Marty fell and where they found him. I wondered where Marty was now. In my mind, he was a good guy — he always waved to me and smiled, and he even invited me down to watch him plow his garden with Nelly that one time.

Later that week, I asked Aunt Erma a lot of questions. I even told her that I had gone into Marty's home and looked in the horse shed. She told me that was wrong, that I had to respect private property and not trespass — that what I did was not respecting Marty. She told me that even if he was a bit different and acted strangely, we needed to respect him. I asked where Nelly was and she told me that a neighbor down the road still farmed with a team of horses and Nelly was at that farm. I asked what happened to Marty and where he was and she told me that folks thought that he had had a heart attack on the way to getting his bucket of water for the day. She also explained about the VA hospital and how veterans who fought in the war were taken care of, and that the VA had a cemetery for veterans who had no family.

I didn't tell her about Nelly plowing the garden or all the waves and smiles Marty shared with me, but I did ask if maybe the next time we went to town, she would take me to the cemetery.

Fine Whisky and Wine

The phone rang at six a.m. on Saturday morning. I'm not an early riser nor a morning person, but I knew my life-long best friend John was, so I wasn't surprised by his call. Every so often, John would show up at our house before nine in the morning with something special to drop off. He would already have been to the public market, had breakfast with his regular group of guys, found all the great deals and bought too much in getting the best price. That's when we were the lucky recipients of some of this bounty. The gifts were usually vegetables and fruits in season but many times, there was a surprise. Once he took me out to his truck and offered a freshly butchered piglet which I politely refused, even after he promised to help barbecue it in a newly built hickory wood fire pit in my lawn. On another occasion, I did accept his offer to show me how to prepare what he called puff balls from a whole basket he had purchased at the market that morning. He cleaned those wild mushrooms, sliced them and fried them in butter and they were a treat for everyone. So, I was familiar with the good and the bad of John's surprises.

On one unforgettable weekend, John called and asked if I was willing to give him a hand for the day. He was my best buddy, so, of course I said I'd be there for him. I asked what was going on and John told me that one of the guys that worked for him was very ill. John had offered to help him at his farm out in Ontario County, but more than one man was needed. I should be ready by nine on Saturday, with four 55-gallon plastic trash cans with lids.

My response was, "What for?"

John simply said, "Just go and buy four trash cans with lids, we'll need them in the morning."

What in the world were we going to do to help this guy out?

A little after nine the following morning, John pulled into my driveway in his work truck — I was ready with the trash cans and with questions. "John, what in hell are we going to do with these trash cans?" He said, "Just put the cans in the back and jump in. It's a long drive and I'll tell you on the way."

En route, he explained. "Sam has cancer and he's worried because he can't harvest his grapes this year. He's a great guy and he's in real trouble so I told him not to worry, that I'd take care of them for him. You and I are going out to his farm to pick the grapes. He makes the grapes into wine so I also told him I'd make his wine for him this year. So, here's the deal: we'll split the grapes, you make half of what we pick into wine for you, and I'll make the other half into wine for Sam."

"But John, I don't even like wine!" John just smiled and looked over at me. "Well then, you can make your wine for me, and I'll pay you for the trash cans. Besides, we'll have a good time helping Sam out. If you really don't want your wine, you can give it to me or give it away to your friends. It will make great gifts for Christmas."

That morning we indeed picked enough to fill four large trash cans with bunches of grapes on the stem leaving several rows untouched. On the way back to my place with the cans in the back of the truck, we stopped for a late lunch which John unexpectedly paid for — I thought perhaps he was feeling a little guilty making me give up a Saturday. That was before I realized I was also about to give up my Sunday.

We unloaded the overflowing cans of grapes into my garage and John said he'd be back tomorrow morning. Sure enough, first thing Sunday morning he pulled into my driveway with a wine press in the back of his truck. "Good morning!" John was full of energy. "I went back to Sam's farm last night and picked up his wine press for us to use today."

We unloaded the press into my garage and spent the rest of the day filling the wooden basket with grapes and then crushing them. After we picked up a cluster and cut off the stem, we'd throw out any spoiled grapes, and then toss the bunch into the wooden basket of the press. When the basket was full, we turned the arm of the screw, collected the juice, and then returned the juice and the grape skins, minus the stems, to the plastic cans. It was a slow process but when we finished, we had four trash cans, each three-quarters filled with grape must, the combination of juice and the crushed solids from the skins and seeds. John told me we would finish up next weekend and, in the meantime, I was to take a clean stick and stir the must, breaking up the top layer on each trash can every day.

"Oh, and just one other thing, before next weekend, make sure you go to Kaplin Barrel Company on River Street in the city and pick up a clean used oak whisky barrel."

The next weekend, when John arrived with his own oak barrel in the back of his truck, my barrel was ready, up on a wooden frame I had built. As always, John was all set to go. "Now we are going to pour the must in the trash cans into the wooden barrels using these funnels and strainers. The whiskey barrels will give the wine a great flavor." By lunchtime, we had finished filling both barrels, one in the back of John's truck and one in my garage. I placed an airlock on the full barrel of juice with instructions to leave it undisturbed. John delivered his barrel to Sam's farm and somehow got it down into the cellar of the farmhouse.

Several weeks went by before John called and told me it was time to rack off my barrel and he'd be over on the weekend to assist. On the phone, he said, "Oh, and just one other thing, pick up eight five-gallon glass carboys."

Saturday came and John helped me set up a siphon system. We carefully drew off the wine in the barrel into the carboys, leaving the sediment undisturbed in the bottom of the barrel. John explained that the wine would continue to clarify, with sediment collecting in the bottom of the carboys. Every few weeks, I was to rack off the clear wine into a new carboy.

When we finally finished the racking process, we had 35 gallons of what was said to be decent wine according to the tasters. By then, there were many of these since the neighbors and other friends had been following our progress, so we decided to have a neighborhood wine party. I still didn't enjoy drinking wine, but I was more than happy to be the bartender for the evening. It was a great party but when it was all over, I still had several full five-gallon carboys of wine left. So, we embarked on bottling and corking. We stored the leftover wine and then gave it away, supplying the wine for all our friend's parties and gatherings. That year, we were the most popular people in our neighborhood.

But there were still many bottles left and I stumbled on an idea. I had not developed a taste for wine, but I did like bubbly drinks. I thought perhaps I could use the wine to make a bubbly wine somewhat like champagne. I read a little, learned about the second fermentation process, and discovered the details of how to carry it out. I located champagne-style yeast, bottles, corks, and wire helmets. I've always been a believer in the philosophy that if a little is good, a little more should be great so while I followed the recipe, I doubled the amount of sugar that I added to start the second fermentation process. As I said, if a little is good...

The freshly modified wine was re-bottled, placed in a cellar cabinet and left for time and nature to work its magic. I checked the bottles weekly, and everything was fine. After a few weeks, my curiosity got the best of me, so I opened a bottle to test it and sure enough, bubbles! Lots of bubbles! Wonderful! I foresaw a spectacular party in the future.

A few more weeks passed and one night as we were sleeping, my wife and I woke to a loud popping noise.

"What is that?" she said.

I replied, "What is what?"

But there was no denying the sounds, one loud pop after another that seemed to be coming from the basement. I raced down to see streams of carbonated wine running out of the cabinet and flowing onto the basement floor. Half the bottles had blown out their corks and since they were lying on their sides, the contents had poured out, making colored streams of wine all over the cellar floor. Clean-up took a considerable amount of time, what with mopping and re-mopping the floor with a cleaning solution.

I wasn't taking any more chances. I retrieved the original, now empty, plastic trash cans from the garage, placed the rest of the still sealed bottles in the cans and hauled them upstairs to the garage. When I checked in the morning, several more bottles had popped their corks, so

I abandoned the idea of a gala party and decided to grace the trash company with both the empty and still sealed bottles.

I started with grapes in new plastic trash cans and ended this saga of wine making with those same trash cans: from trash can to trash as the saying goes... oh sorry, that's a different saying. As for the wooden whiskey barrel, I sawed it in half. We used one half to store wood for the fireplace in our family room and the other half for the wood stove at our cabin. We continued to enjoy the ever so faint aroma of fine whiskey and wine for years.

Christmas Kitchen Memories

Maybe I remember the popcorn balls best because of all the smells. Handfuls of popping corn tossed into the hot lard in the cast iron skillet on the wood stove hissed and sputtered as the smell of the popping corn slid out from under the lid. A powerful cloud of sugar hung over the bubbling pot of dyed-red corn syrup. Everyone was called to the kitchen to help when large bowls of popcorn lined the kitchen table, waiting for the hot syrup. Just as the last popcorn was added, the hot, sweet syrup was poured over each bowl. Armed with big wooden spoons, we made sure every kernel was completely coated. Then quickly, quickly before the syrup could set, every helping hand was covered with butter and each pair of hands grabbed a big handful of the syrup-coated popped corn to make their own balls. The ideal size was as big as a softball!

All the finished popcorn balls were piled on a platter, stacked to a high pyramid to be enjoyed throughout the holiday season. With every bite, corn and syrup stuck to your teeth like glue but they tasted so good it didn't seem to matter that you had to chew and chew and chew some more. Even the pain from the attack of an un-popped kernel was no impediment — they were just that good.

That same wood stove was used to make the best fudge in the world. The recipe was on the back of the Hershey powdered cocoa can, but enhanced by the use of fresh, high-fat farm butter and cow's milk with just a pinch more salt and perhaps an extra spoon of cocoa. Help was called for in the kitchen for three very important tasks. Little fingers were needed to carefully spread butter all over the big platter so the fudge wouldn't stick as it cooled. Bigger fingers were needed to open walnuts with a nutcracker and remove the meat so that it could be added to the fudge after it had finished cooking. The last important task was to have volunteers clean out the empty cooking pan with wooden spoons — there was never a problem finding willing helpers for this delicious chore! The creamy fudge just melted in your mouth, the chocolate enhanced by just a hint of the extra salted butter. Delicious!!

Baked Christmas cookies from the wood stove oven with anise frosting came in every rainbow color and Christmas-themed shape. One of the fun tasks was helping to pick out the cookie cutters to be used: the first unanimous choice was always Santa followed by the Christmas tree. All the others didn't seem to matter that much. Each pair of helping hands was given a bowl of white frosting and little bottles of food coloring were placed in the middle of the table. Stirred with a knife, bowls of rainbow colors emerged to be shared by everyone. Colored sugar sprinkles were provided, and then little busy hands frosted the stacks of cookies and added the sprinkles. The standing rule was that if you broke one it had to be eaten and only the perfect ones were to be placed on the trays. Now that's a good rule!

The cook stove in the kitchen had a huge appetite. First thing in the morning, the empty wood box in the back room always had to be filled. Dressed in warm work clothes and boots, we kids carried armful after armful of wood from the pile out by the barn near the buzz saw into the back room. The wood was heavy, and the trip seemed longer with each round. When it surely felt like time to quit, the wood box "inspector" always asked for just two more armfuls to fill it up all the way to the "tippy top." By the time we finished, we were completely soaked.

All the wet clothes and mittens and socks were hung with clothes pins on wires behind the stove to dry: the smell of wet wool was omnipresent, all winter long. Cold and hungry, the perfect warm-up came from standing around that kitchen stove with a cup of hot chocolate and a Christmas cookie with extra thick frosting and sugar sprinkles.

I Don't Know if it Happened This Way . . .

Johanna

I grew up not knowing how blessed I was to have been able to interact with many strong, independent, creative and loving women while I was young. These were women who taught me so many of life's joys and lessons. I was not aware of their influence until much later in my life. One particular case in point was Johanna Rightmire, the wife of my grandmother's older brother, Carl. Johanna was my great aunt, but she was also my mother's aunt. Johanna, her husband Carl, and my grandmother were all born in the late 1800's and I was generations apart from them but we always connected well with each other.

My mother would often say to me and my grandmother, "Let's go down to Aunt Johanna's this weekend." My grandmother would come along with us for these visits since it was an opportunity for her to see her brother Carl and her sister-in-law, Johanna. I always called them Aunt Johanna and Uncle Carl because my mother naturally did. They lived on a farm in Pennsylvania near the small rural hamlet of Proctor: the entire community had one general store, one church, a one-room schoolhouse, and perhaps ten homes. One of the houses was the Rightmire homestead where Carl and his brother and sisters were born and raised.

Proctor has faded over time since what the locals referred to as its "heyday," back when Carl was a boy. Today, Proctor can be found on a map of Pennsylvania on County Route 3, surrounded by four massive Loyalsock forest preserves. Route 3 is not listed as a secondary road but rather its designation is found among "other selected roads." To call it rural is giving it the full benefit of the doubt. Although now standing empty, Proctor's original church and the schoolhouse with its separate outhouses for boys and girls are still maintained. The original general store, however, is still open for business. This area is often referred to as, "the endless mountains of Pennsylvania." The cultural, financial, and commercial center of this central part of the state, the city of Williamsport, is 40 miles to the south, beyond the mountains.

Carl and Johanna's farm was a five mile walk from Proctor's general store. To reach the farm, there was a long, steep dirt road which began at the narrow, paved road which led out of town over the mountain towards Forksville. The road to the farm was literally hand built by Carl with his own pure muscle and his team of horses. It must have been back-breaking work. The road ended at the farm on top of the hill, three thousand feet straight up the mountain. A car or truck could only make it up the road by crawling slowly in low gear. Many times, I walked down this road — euphemistically called the driveway — to the mailbox at the end and then back up again. In addition to the mail, there were also usually packages in the extra-large mailbox, since much of the shopping was done through the mail in those days, ordered from the Sears Roebuck or Montgomery Ward catalogues. I was always totally breathless by the time I got back up to the farmhouse.

The 50-acre farm had no electricity or running water until the early 1950's with the advent of the Federal Rural Electrification Act (REA). Undaunted, Johanna raised her family there, often entirely on her own: this meant she milked the cows; made butter and canned vegetables, fruit and meat; slaughtered animals in the fall; did all the laundry by hand; and managed all the finances. The farmhouse Carl and Johanna lived in was, in its first life, actually a logging camp built in the hamlet of Proctor during the time when virgin forests were being harvested and sawmills were the main business for the area. Carl was a logger most of his working life while also managing the farm. As a young man, he was even the school master in Proctor! After the lumber business left the township of Proctor, Carl traveled west by train to earn money, often for months at a time. While he was gone, Johanna was left to run the farm entirely by herself, a testament to her formidable independence and strength.

Early in their married life, Carl and Johanna bought the farm property and it was then that Carl built the road to the top of the mountain. When the lumber company abandoned Proctor and moved on to harvest other forest areas in the state, an abandoned logging camp dormitory in Proctor became available. Carl and Johanna were the highest bidders and together, they proceeded to dismantle the building board by board, load the lumber in their wagon, and pulled by their team of horses, haul it five miles out of town and up the mountain road to the farm. Carl and Johanna actually dug the cellar and foundation for the building by hand(!) and then re-erected the old dormitory building on the new site. This was followed by the construction of a barn, several outbuildings and a workshop.

The old dormitory/new farmhouse was a two-story building, with the lower floor divided into two large rooms. One room was the original kitchen/eating area for the men and the other was a communal room where the loggers used to relax in the evenings. The second floor consisted of two small bedrooms and one large room for the loggers' bunks. As a child, I remember the original kitchen area for the loggers was still used as the kitchen for the farmhouse. It contained a wood cook stove, a wood box, a table which could accommodate a dozen place settings, floor to ceiling cupboards, and what the family referred to as a 'day bed,' a broad hand-built wooden shelf attached to the wall near the stove. The stove had 'wells' on each side for water which was heated when the fire burned. This was the only hot water available for Johanna to use to wash dishes and do laundry, and it was the only hot water available for bathing, in a round tin tub on the back porch. The stove was used for all cooking and baking, so it was in active use all day long. Johanna would rise at five in the morning, start the fire, heat water in the coffee pot and cook breakfast so it was ready and on the table at 6 am. After the breakfast dishes were washed, she baked bread along with a variety of cookies, pies, and what I remember best, cinnamon rolls. Perhaps, starting breakfast at five in the morning was part of a plan on how to survive the hot summer weather. The required task of baking was usually reserved for the cooler days of the week. When I think about all this, I continue to be amazed by the number of day-to-day activities required to run the household and the farm — all completed by my aunt, Johanna.

In the kitchen, a wall divided the ground floor in the middle, with doors at either end, separating it from the great room on the other side. During the colder months of the year, the farmhouse was heated only by the cook stove in the kitchen and a small wood stove in the great room. Both doors leading into the great room were kept closed during the day so the kitchen was always warm and cozy from the heat of the cook stove. The only heat in the upstairs bedrooms was provided by a pipe from the stove in the great room, which went through the ceiling to the upstairs and ran the entire length of the communal bedroom near the ceiling to a chimney on the other end of the house.

Most of the family's evening activities took place in the kitchen and these included candy-making, preparing and drying fruit, cracking hickory nuts, card and board games, or just sitting around visiting. Scrabble was the favorite board game and card games included Hearts, Spades and Pinochle. I can still recall the wonderful smells in that kitchen when we visited. If it was a baking day, the aroma of yeast prepared you for the fresh baked bread that would welcome you in a few hours. Breakfast aromas of bacon frying, along with eggs and fried potatoes greeted you each morning. Fudge cooking on the stove always made my mouth water. Fresh baked pies cooling on the cupboard alerted me to clean my plate at the next meal. I thought to myself, if there was a heaven, it couldn't be any better than this.

During dinner conversation in the cooler months, the evening activity was usually selected. As a preliminary, Aunt Johanna would suggest to Uncle Carl that he start a fire in the stove in the living room. When the room was warm and comfortable, guests and family would settle in for the evening to read, visit, or listen to the radio. Saturday night's entertainment was provided by the radio tuned to the Grand Old Opry, if reception was clear and the battery had enough charge. A gas-lit chandelier provided good reading light over the kitchen table while the great room was lit by kerosene lamps. Bedtime required carrying a lamp up the dark stairs to the sleeping area, quickly extinguished as soon as you climbed into bed.

When we visited on the weekends, I was always assigned tasks by Aunt Johanna. These included keeping the wood box in the kitchen filled, refilling the oil lamps each morning, hand cranking the cream-separator machine on the back porch after the cows were milked, taking the garbage pail out to the pen to feed the hogs, and returning to the kitchen to turn the hand crank on the butter jar to whip the cream into butter. My reward was usually a couple of warm cinnamon buns with lunch. These tasks assigned by my aunt always made me feel important and needed — I felt as if I was really helping around the farm when we visited, even perhaps justifying the extra burden of additional mouths to feed and beds to sleep in.

The wood for the kitchen stove was stored in a separate building located about 25 feet from the back porch. Since the stove burned all day long, the wood box never seemed to be completely filled so I never had time to be bored. Two-gallon cans of kerosene were stored on the back porch and in filling the oil lamps, I had to be very careful not to spill any oil. The glass chimneys of the lamps had to be cleaned before filling the bowls, done best by using newspaper to rub off the carbon silt. Next on the list was feeding the chickens. I would gather a pail of dried corn on the cob from the corn crib and after carefully latching the door behind me, walk over to the workshop where the corn sheller sat on the porch. Feeding the cobs into the machine and turning the crank by hand sent the kernels out the bottom into the bucket and the clean cobs shooting out the other side at the top of the machine. I fed the kernels of corn to the chickens and the second bucket of cobs to the hogs. One day, I asked Aunt Johanna who did all the chores when I wasn't there. She just looked at me and smiled. This made me feel special and very much needed.

On special weekends when all the work for the day was done, Johanna would suggest that maybe we should go fishing and "get a mess of trout" for dinner. Johanna always knew where to go and usually suggested we try "the little Loyalsock Creek." Aunt Johanna taught me how to fly fish, and the proper way to bait a hook. Depending on the time of year, she also taught me which fly hook to use, including the correct feather color. She taught me how to hold the bamboo pole, how to send the line back and forth above my head, and how to pick the right spot to land the bait above the whirlpool, before letting it drift down the stream. She showed me how to not block the sunlight so my shadow would never show on the water. When we had caught our limit, she taught me how to clean the fish and prepare them for frying, how much grease to put in the cast iron frying pan and how to tell when the pan was hot enough to drop in the trout. Instructions also included how to tell when the trout were perfectly cooked so the fish slid cleanly off the bones, how to fry potatoes in another pan at the same time and how to have them finish cooking at the exact same moment. That was my Aunt Johanna. I think of her to this day when I once again re-use some part of all this knowledge.

One fall weekend when we were visiting, Aunt Johanna asked me to go to the cellar and bring up a quart jar of canned meat so she could prepare lunch for us. When I returned and told her the shelf was empty, she said something like, "Well, we'll have to take care of that. I'll figure out what else we'll have for lunch instead." I was sent out to the garden to pick tomatoes while Aunt Johanna fried up some of her farm bacon and then I had the best tomato sandwich I ever tasted. After the lunch dishes were washed, dried, and put away, Aunt Johanna took the .22 rifle out of the gun cabinet, told me she was going for a walk and that I should stay near the house and not wander off. Later that afternoon, I saw her walking down through the hay field from the far woods, carrying the rifle in her hand with a small deer hanging over her shoulders. When she reached the back porch, I realized she had already cleaned it. She told me she had to take care of it right away because it was a little too warm that day to leave it overnight. Then she asked me if I knew how to prepare a deer for eating. I learned a lot that day.

That was my Aunt Johanna, strong, independent, creative, and loving.

Reflecting on these visits over the years and how much all this imprinted my life, I realize now how difficult life was for the generations in my family that came before me and how easy my own life has been in comparison. I remember the rare times that Aunt Johanna would come out of the kitchen to the large porch which ran across the entire front of the house, facing down the hill towards the path along the creek to the barn. Aunt Johanna would sit next to me on one of the many rocking chairs. She always had her apron on — never took it off — and we would just rock back and forth in our own chairs. She would look out at the horses and the barn below and always say, "Isn't that just the most peaceful and beautiful thing that you ever saw?" I don't think at the time I understood what was so peaceful and beautiful. Now I reflect on the thousands of times she walked up that path from the barn carrying two buckets of milk, down that path carrying two other buckets to feed the hogs, and the many trips to the barn she made, to hook up the horses to the hay fork or to help Carl unload the hay from the wagon and into the lofts — thousands of trips, whatever the weather. I also try to think what it must have been like for her to look up that steep hill while sitting on the horse drawn wagon filled with lumber for her new home, dreaming of the finished building and her future life. Indeed, it must have been a beautiful and peaceful time for her to sit and rock on that front porch with me years later and relax just a bit before going back to the kitchen to prepare dinner for all her guests and her husband. I can still hear her saying, "Gary — would you mind going in and sticking a few pieces of wood into the stove and taking the water bucket out to the well and filling it up and bringing it in, while I sit here and rock a bit more?"

That was my Aunt Johanna, born in the 1800's! I think I'm going to go and sit and rock a bit and reflect on how beautiful, peaceful, and easy my own life has been.

The Elusive Cup

The secret to gourmet, silky smooth, dark chocolate fudge is one cup of hickory nuts added to the recipe on the back of the 1940s Hershey's Special Dark Cocoa container. That recipe read:

2/3 cup Hershey's Cocoa or Hershey's Special Dark Cocoa

3 cups sugar

1/8 teaspoon salt

1-1/2 cups milk

1/4 cup butter

1 teaspoon vanilla extract

For nutty rich cocoa fudge: beat cooked fudge as directed. Immediately stir in 1 cup of chopped almonds, pecans, or walnuts and spread quickly in prepared pan.

* * * * * * * *

Notice that hickory nuts are not listed among the choice of nuts. That is because they are difficult to acquire and usually not available for sale except as the whole unshelled nut. So, obtaining a cup of hickory nuts is a challenge. But the hunt is worth the effort as the nut provides an unusual, earthy, and delightful taste in dark chocolate fudge.

Hickory trees are rare and hard to find in hardwood forests of the Northeast. A hundred or more years ago, farmers realized that hickory trees provided another food source for their families. The nuts were used in baking, in cooking recipes and for winter evening snacks around the fireplace or wood stove. In the fall when the nuts ripened and dropped from the trees, farmers would assign their family members to pick them up from the ground and peel off their thick outer hulls. The collected nuts were then taken to the farmhouse where they were spread out on the floor in the attic to dry for several months.

Removing the inside or the 'meat' of the nut is a trial of strength, endurance, perseverance and skill, an art few individuals ever achieve. The shell of the nut is best cracked by being held tightly between the thumb and forefinger on a piece of heavy thick steel and then striking the nut in just the perfect spot with a heavy hammer. Hickory nuts look like miniature walnuts although they are much smaller and narrower in the middle. The insides of both nuts are also similar in that, when split open, there are two separate halves, and the 'meat' must be picked out of each half shell by hand. That is where the similarity ends.

The meat of the walnut comes out fairly easily unless the shell is broken unevenly when the meat must be dug out with metal tools or picks. By contrast, it is rare to have a hickory nut break evenly and neatly into two equal halves — that takes real skill and experience. Unfortunately, the effort to crack the hard shell often results in a misjudgment of the force required by the hammer, with the end result of hitting your own thumb and finger as the shell finally gives way. At this juncture, new words are usually added to the conversation of friends or family tasked with trying to gather the required cup of nuts gathered around the table. All the while, the fudge continues quietly bubbling away on the cast iron wood stove in the kitchen.

I was introduced to fudge with hickory nuts as a young lad when my Great Aunt Johanna asked me if I wanted her to make me some fudge. Great Aunt Johanna and Great Uncle Carl lived on a farm on top of one of the high hills in Pennsylvania. They heated their farmhouse with wood, farmed with a team of horses, used kerosene lamps, made maple syrup from their maple trees and collected the afore-mentioned hickory nuts from their own trees.

One cold and snowy evening in December when I was about 12 years old, the after-dinner conversation went something like this...

Great Aunt Johanna: "How would you like me to make you some fudge tonight?"

"Great!"

GAJ: "You'll have some work to do if you want fudge."

"OK!"

GAJ: "OK then, take this bowl up to the attic and scoop up enough nuts off the floor to fill it. Then go out to the woodshed — you'll find a short piece of railroad rail and bring it in. Then go to Uncle Carl's shop and bring in three carpenter hammers."

I was off like a circus clown shot from a cannon and was soon back with my arms loaded. Then the "fun" began. Uncle Carl and Aunt Joanna joined in cracking the bowl of nuts, trying to teach me exactly how best to hold the nut, how hard to hit it, and how to pick out the 'meat' from the broken shell. Since the nuts are so small and the shell so hard, broken bits are a common result of cracking efforts. Broken bits of shell, however tiny, must be avoided at all costs since biting down on an errant piece can break a tooth. Digging the meat out with a pick is also most difficult — hence the effort to split the nut cleanly in half without splitting your thumb or finger with the hammer. A cup may not seem like much until such time as you have a pile of nuts on the table in front of you and a one-and-a-half-pound hammer in your hand.

Trust me, that nut fudge tasted like a bit of heaven. And it turns out, one can still appreciate the world's most delicious nut fudge even with a Band-Aid on your finger or your thumb or both. Alas, they continued to throb long after the last delicious piece of fudge was gone.

George's Ham Sandwich

The massive engine's single bright light pierced the darkness like an arrow pierces its paper target. The engineer focused on the green light from the semaphore signal trackside and then checked the steam pressure gauge before he slowly bumped the throttle handle one click forward. He checked his pocket watch and hollered over to his fireman, "Shovel that %$# coal faster so we can build up some pressure. We have a schedule to keep and we're running late!" Both men were totally unaware of the fate that awaited them further up the line.

The Erie railroad tracks ran along the banks of the shallow rocky bottom of the Canisteo River which meandered like a rattlesnake through the valley. For thousands of years, the yearly spring flooding of the river provided rich, flat, bottom farmland. The fields within the valley were bounded on both sides by steep wooded hills, sculpted by glaciers eons ago. The farm families that tilled this land lived in well-kept, freshly painted houses. The barns with their whitewashed milking basements beneath mammoth hay lofts under gambrel roofs were the mainstay of the family farm. There was not a lot of money to be made from the monthly milk check or from boiling maple sap and making syrup and sugar to sell in the spring. But there was always enough to feed the family: milk, cream, butter and meat from the cows and eggs from free-range chickens.

The land between the high hills was commonly referred to as the 'river bottom' by the local folks. The railroad tracks and the narrow country road ran parallel through the towns situated along their length every ten miles or so, passing through Addison, Cameron Mills, and Cameron before the tracks connected with the Lackawanna Railroad further down the line. Where the river wound back and forth across the valley, old one-lane rickety steel bridges supported the occasional car or tractor to its destination. In most towns, one could find a general store or two, a one- or two-room schoolhouse, a Protestant church, once in a while a Catholic church, a Grange Hall, and almost always, a Masonic Hall. Most folks never talked about it, but in and around Cameron, the message in three 10-foot-high capital Ks painted on the sheer rock cliffs above the town was very clear. Unless you are one of us, keep out of this valley — you are not welcome here!

Beyond the river, one's view was of birches, with maples further up and a few struggling hemlocks covering the hills as far as the eye could see. Life was not easy and everyone worked long, hard hours to survive. There was always enough to eat but other than the check for milk, there wasn't much additional income unless one worked for the Erie or Lackawanna railroads and those jobs were few and far between.

George lived on one of those farms. As a young preteen, in addition to helping in the barn, at harvest time, and maple sugaring, his primary chore consisted of keeping the family warm in the winter. After school and before dark, George would walk the railroad tracks to pick up the scattered coal dropped by the hopper cars when the coal freight trains ran along this main route. The coal was used to augment winter wood fires and to build a 'keeper fire' for those long cold nights when a howling wind blew through the valley, dumping large amounts of snow. The old farmhouse had no insulation and snow blew in under the clapboards and through cracks around the windows and doors right into the house. The buckets of coal from the tracks provided a hot and lasting fire in the evening and right through the night. And the coal was there for the taking. True, as the picking got thinner, the walks along the tracks got longer and longer and the bucket grew heavier and heavier. But the found and picked coal was a lot less work in the long run than using the cross-cut or buck saw and ax to split the logs piled up by the barn for firewood.

Life was very routine until fate intervened on the night of February 13, 1930. George and his mom, dad, younger brother, and sister were tucked in for the night while the burning coal in the stove gave off toasty heat for all. Meanwhile, the Erie engineer was making up for lost time with the throttle bumped up one notch. Suddenly, with no warning whatsoever, the focused light illuminated the distant rear of a red caboose with a swinging red lantern held by a brakeman on the side of the tracks. The freight train ahead was stopped and standing still on the same track as this oncoming train! Too late, the engineer hit the brakes and pulled the reverse lever on the engine. Too late, the engine's wheels were sliding and sparks were flying, but the weight and momentum of all the cars just kept pushing the engine and the whole train ahead. Time ran out. Distance ran out. The engine slammed into the rear of the stalled train ahead. The noise was deafening, as several cars were forced off the track. Some broke loose and tumbled down the embankment, bursting open and spilling their contents along the way.

The sounds of the wreck woke everyone. George was dressed and out of the house in a flash. And what to his amazement did he see in the beam of his flashlight... burst wooden train cars full of Hormel canned hams with even more cans scatted all along the tracks. Many of the five-pound cans were not even dented. His first trip home was with an armful of those five pounders — all he could carry, each fifty pounds! The next few trips he carried a bit less, since running was so taxing, and being out of breath made each trip a bit harder. But, by the time he needed to get ready for school, the pantry was stocked full with more canned hams than Bart's General Store in Cameron could have possibly sold in a year.

As the only boy who lived close to the wreck, George was a local hero at school that day. He warned his buddies and swore them to secrecy to never say a word of this ever, and for sure to promise him that when the railroad detectives arrived and asked any questions about the missing canned hams, they would say nothing because he didn't want to go to Attica Prison. George's mother had a bit of a problem with the new-found tins in her pantry as she was a God-fearing, church-going Christian lady, but then, she couldn't remember the last time the family had a canned ham, let alone a ham sandwich with mustard on thick homemade bread. And just think what this could mean for George's school lunches!

No detectives ever knocked on any farm home doors after the accident. There was no mention of Hormel hams or for that matter, any hams at all in the local paper. No one, it seemed, was interested in any canned Hormel hams. The stories in the paper were only about the cause of the wreck and why the other train was stopped on the tracks. But for the rest of his life, George never liked canned ham, or any Hormel products at all, for that matter... imagine that!

Just One Little Bottle Was All That Was Needed

The old farmhouse sat a long way back from both the road and the driveway. A deep snow drift blocked the driveway's entrance and the driver of the car had to decide whether to plow through the drift or simply park on the side of the road, necessitating a long, cold hike through the deep snow. A trial plunge into the drift was deemed preferable, so the driver backed up the road to get some speed and then drove headfirst into the drift. An explosion of flying snow immediately covered the windshield: all the driver and passengers could see was a dense, white cloud as the rear wheels spun out of control and the car lurched and bucked through the drift. There was a cacophony of sound as spinning tires threw gravel against the fenders. Slowly, slowly, the car inched forward before finally breaking free from the deep snow and stopping in the driveway between the barn and the house.

There was still the hike to the house so the family buttoned up their coats, pulled their hats down over their ears, put on their gloves, picked up all the wrapped presents from the trunk and trudged through the deep snow to the steps of the back porch. Once in the kitchen, they stamped their feet on the door mat to shake off the snow and gathered around the wood stove to warm their hands and feet. All the little kids, eyes as big as saucers, stared at the presents piled on the day bed near the stove but then they rushed, excited, past the presents to cluster around their cousin from the city with one big question:

"Did you bring the bottle of pills?"

"Yes, I told you I would."

"Can we see them?"

"Here they are, right here."

"C'mon, let's try them out!"

"OK!"

"Let's go — we have the whole setup ready back here in the playroom."

The children followed their older cousin as if he were the Pied Piper, through the kitchen, into the living room and then into the playroom. The living room was the only part of the house that had a full basement under it and was therefore fairly warm. All the other rooms had only crawl spaces beneath them — this plus no insulation meant the rooms were ice cold and the floors even colder. The playroom had flower-patterned linoleum and in the far corner, a pot-bellied wood stove that was barely able to heat the room to a balmy sixty degrees. You would think it almost impossible to sit on that ice cold floor, but the kids flung themselves down in excited anticipation of seeing those little pills work. The last time they watched the magic of the pills was weeks ago and to these kiddos, it felt like forever.

A complete Lionel electric train set was all ready to go. The oldest child plugged in the transformer, pulled the controller lever down a little and the steam engine locomotive and its attached cars began to move slowly around the track. The "engineer" stopped at the automatic log loader and the log car was loaded. Next stop was the depot and the box car was loaded automatically with milk cans. As the engine and cars moved around the track, the railroad crossing lights flashed red, on and off. But the best was yet to come...

"Stop right here in front of me so I can put a smoke pellet in the stack."

"Put two or three in."

"No, you are only supposed to put one in at a time."

"OK, OK. Start it up. Let's see if it works!"

"Look at that!"

Little round puffs of white smoke emerged from the smokestack as the Lionel 027 gauge steam engine with its headlight shining on the track chugged ahead and the train made its way around the layout and through the little town. It was magic! One tiny bottle of Lionel Smoke Pellets made a marvelous Christmas celebration for those farm kids. For a moment, everyone even forgot the big pile of wrapped presents in the kitchen. The next morning, all attention would be on those presents under the tree. But for now, the tiny bottle of pills and the puffs of smoke were all the children needed for a perfect Christmas Eve.

I Don't Know if it Happened This Way . . .

Cloverine

I clearly remember that day. I was 12 years old and had just finished reading the latest issue of my friend's DC comic book, The Adventures of Superman. There it was, in brilliant color on the back page of the comic: a full-page advertisement for the Wilson Chemical Company in Tyrone, PA offering cash or premiums if you sent for their BIG free catalogue! Drawings of some of the free gifts included a boy's or girl's bike, a matching knife and hatchet set, a .22 caliber rifle, a BB gun, a radio, a flashlight, a telescope, a camera, a cuckoo clock, and even a live pony! There was a comic strip to go with the ad, and below the drawings in each pane were these accompanying words:

"HELP! The gorilla is loose!"

"Stand back! I've got a gun!"

"Look! He's climbing back into his cage! That boy and girl saved our lives!"

"You kids deserve a medal! Where did you get the .22 rifle and the bow and arrow?"

"We earned them selling WHITE CLOVERINE BRAND SALVE!"

"Wow! I'm gonna sell some of that salve, too!"

I was hooked. Quickly, I found a pencil and filled out the form at the bottom of the page which read, "MAIL NOW. BIG CATALOG! Gentleman, Please send me on trial 14 colorful art pictures with 14 boxes of White CLOVERINE brand SALVE to sell at 35 cents a box (with picture). I will remit amount asked within 30 days, select a Premium or keep Cash Commission as explained under Premium wanted in the catalog sent with the order, postage paid to start." Right at the bottom where I printed my name it said, "WE ARE RELIABLE!" How in the world could I go wrong? I was finally going to have my own BB gun and all I had to do was sell 56 boxed tins of Cloverine Salve! How hard could that be?

I searched the house for an envelope and a stamp and finally had to ask Grandma for her help, prompting an inquiry from her. I hedged a bit and finally, had to tell a little white lie. Well, let's face it... I had to tell her a real lie as I already knew I would not be allowed to have a BB gun. But Grandma gave me a stamp and an envelope. I placed the form in the envelope, ran out to the mailbox and put up the flag. Every day after school, I checked the mailbox for my package. Day after day there was nothing. Finally, after what seemed as long a time as waiting for Christmas to come after Thanksgiving was over, there it was, a long tube with my very own name on it, beginning with Mr! Mr. Gary Buehler! I ran into the house, cut open the tube and pulled out 14 little boxes, each containing a tin of Cloverine Salve. Also inside the tube were 14 rolled up printed posters of Jesus to be given as gifts to each purchaser, along with a list of all the benefits and uses for the salve. The last item in the tube was the catalog of prizes. It was breathtakingly beautiful!

I found the page for the BB gun. I could barely contain my delight: I only had to sell three more tubes of salve after this batch to qualify for the gun. At dinner, I excitedly showed off my 14 tins of salve and the page from the catalog for the BB gun. Once again, it was confirmed that I could not have a BB gun until I was older. I spent the evening studying the catalog and finally came to the conclusion that the bow and arrow set would be almost as good as the BB gun — and I only had to sell two more tubes of salve instead of three. What could be easier?

It only took me a week to sell all 14 tins in that first tube. My grandmother bought two, each of my aunts and uncles bought one, most of my neighbors bought one, and all my mother's friends bought one. Per the signed agreement, I had to send $3.50 back to the Wilson Chemical Company in order to receive my second tube. Of course, I could have kept $1.40 as cash profit but it was an easy decision: even if I sold three tubes and kept all the cash, I knew I couldn't buy a bow and arrow set anywhere near where I lived for $4.20. I rode my bike to the post office and mailed the letter off, along with the money order.

A week later, my second tube arrived but this time, some of the excitement was gone. Now I was faced with finding new customers further down the street who were strangers to me. As my sales territory expanded, much more walking and knocking on doors was needed. Finally, my second payment was mailed to the company and the third tube arrived. This time, there was no excitement — I mean, none at all. Again, I had to expand my sales area. I began almost begging, telling folks I just had to sell this last tube of salve in order to get my prize. Occasionally, this approach engendered some sympathy from older ladies and even a few successful sales, but they were few and far between. In the end, I had to ask my grandmother for a "loan" of $3.50 to send to the company. I promised I would pay her back when I sold all the remaining tins.

Happily, I rode my bike to the post office, bought another money order and stamp, and mailed the envelope off to the Wilson Chemical Company, along with my selected premium from the catalog. Enthusiasm rose again as I waited for my premium to arrive. Every day, I jumped off the school bus, hoping to see a package in our mailbox. Finally, after almost two weeks, there it was: as I climbed down the steps of the bus, I could see a long tube protruding from the box. And the tube was addressed to me, Mr. Gary Buehler!!! It felt like Christmas morning all over again! Bounding through the back door into the kitchen, I grabbed a knife and ripped open the end of the tube. Inside, I found a wooden bow with a paper target wrapped around the center and three wooden arrows. Each arrow had red feathers on the shaft and a small metal point on the arrowhead. I ran outside, attached the string to the bow, placed an arrow in my hand and pointed it at the garage door. Zing. It hit the door — excellent! It left a mark — not so good. Clearly, using the bow would need some practice.

Over dinner, I shared my excitement with the family and hardly taking time to chew, finished quickly. Outside, Johnny Pots from across the street noticed my new addition and came running over to try it out. We put the paper target on a cardboard box and began shooting, trying to hit the bull's eye. Soon we were bored because after only three shots, we had to run and gather up all the arrows that had missed the target and the box all together. Johnny suggested that we try to see how high in the sky we could shoot an arrow. Great idea, I thought. So, pulling the string back as far as I could, I let the arrow fly. High up into the sky and then an ever so slight arc and back to earth it came, faster and faster, finally burying itself deeply in the grass of the lawn. My buddy Johnny shouted, "Great shot! Try another one but higher this time!" I pulled back with all my might and let this one fly, almost out of sight. We spotted it coming down... "Oh nooo!!" Johnny shouted. There was a slight ting and then the red feathers were all that was left, sticking out of my mother's brand new 1953 Chevrolet, smack dab in the middle of the roof. Inside the car, I saw the point of the arrowhead had penetrated right through the roof and the shaft was now almost to the top of the front seat.

Johnny said, "I have to go home now," and disappeared. I was left with the carnage. I reached inside the car, grabbed the wooden shaft and pushed it straight up to the cloth headliner. Up on the roof, I pulled the arrow shaft the rest of the way out. Back inside, I sat down and looked up at the roof... nothing! To my amazement, the cloth didn't even show a hole! But what if it rains? Casually, I strolled inside and asked my grandma for two sticks of her Beech-Nut Gum. Outside, I chewed the gum like crazy. When it was just the right consistency, I reached over to the center of the roof, stuck it into the hole and smoothed it out with my finger. Bingo! Problem solved.

One thing about my mother was that she loved cars — she bought a new one every two or three years during her entire lifetime. A shiny new, good looking, sporty car in mint condition was always one of her prized possessions. But, at 12 years old, I thought she never knew anything about that errant arrow and the hole in the roof. Many years later, at her 80th birthday party in our family church, I had the opportunity to tell this story to all her friends and family present assembled for the celebration. Mom listened carefully and smiled when I finished, before she said, "Why I never knew that!" To this day, I'm not convinced that wasn't a little white lie... and in church no less!

Several years after the 1953 Chevy and a few new cars later, we moved and many tins of Cloverine were packed and then unpacked and placed in the medicine cabinet in the bathroom of our new home. Those tins remained there for years, long after I moved out. The $3.50 loan to grandma was never repaid but she did claim all the left-over tins and advised everyone to use the salve for cuts, scrapes, burns, bug bites, sun burn, dry skin, to remove wrinkles, and, even, to put a dab under your nose to avoid a cold. Grandma practiced what she preached and used Cloverine on herself and all the grandkids for years. She never ran out of tins of salve!

As a footnote to history, by the 1930s, three hundred thousand young kids were selling Cloverine salve and the Wilson Chemical Company had so many sales requests and orders to ship that it had to have its own postal substation established at Cloverine Terrace near the Company's headquarters in Tyrone, PA. In 1967, the Federal Trade Commission determined that the company's advertising methods of luring young salespeople had to stop and ordered it to do so. The catalogs, old tins, religious prints, and vintage ads are now highly collectable. I sure would like to have just one of those original tins from Grandma's medicine cabinet, just for the memory, and to smell it once again.

The Big Toe

I should have stopped to think about my idea of a practical joke and considered the possible consequences of my actions, but at 13, like many teens, I didn't think. As a much older and hopefully wiser adult, I know that in the brains of teenagers, the amygdala guides immediate reactions rather than the frontal cortex which controls reasoning and helps us to think before we act. On this fateful evening, my 13-year-old amygdala was engaged but the frontal cortex was not. As I planned this practical joke, there was actually no reasoning taking place at all, not one iota.

On the other hand, my dear uncle George, was no doubt, not engaged in any brain activity either, other than deep REM sleep. He had walked up from the barn after milking his herd of cows to have a late dinner and grab a few winks on the day bed in the kitchen by the warm wood stove — a short break, sorely needed before returning to the barn to finish feeding the cows, heifers, and calves, and cleaning the stalls and gutters before finally calling it a night.

A bit of insight and background may assist in understanding better why this practical joke was such a bad idea. It was a mere nine years after Uncle George returned home from WWII. The conflict took a terrible toll on him which I never even began to understand until I was an adult myself, reflecting on his life. My uncle enlisted in the Army in January 1941, before Pearl Harbor brought America into the war and remained in the Army through the duration of WWII before finally being discharged in 1945. He was a heavy machine-gunner and served in the

Western Pacific in many of the major battles, including the assault on the Gilbert and Marshall Islands, Saipan, and Okinawa, among others. Those years took a major toll.

Back to me, age 13. When my uncle returned from the barn and before we all sat down to dinner, my Aunt Erma had been vacuuming the kitchen floor. After dinner was over, as I indicated, my uncle lay down for a short rest. My aunt told me to be quiet until he woke up while she returned to the living room to entertain the children and hopefully keep them from being too noisy. I sat at the table and looked at the vacuum cleaner — the long hose, the shiny, stainless-steel tube at the end — and then, glancing over at my uncle's bare feet in front of the stove, I wondered if that tube would fit over his big toe. I bet myself it would, and I bet I could do it without waking him up! Never once did I think of the consequences — actually, never once did I think at all, except to bet myself I could pull this stunt off.

I won the bet! I slipped the chrome tube over his big toe ever so slowly and carefully, with one hand on the tube. With my other hand, I hit the switch on the blue and chrome Electrolux sitting on the floor. There was a flutter of the big toe as the vacuum came alive followed immediately by a deep, gut level, blood-curdling cry. My uncle sprang awake — but he was clearly in a different time and place. He bolted upright in a hunched position, his feet planted firmly on top of the bed with an imaginary knife in one hand and his machine gun in the other. As Aunt Erma and the children came running into the room, my uncle stood frozen, transfixed, staring at the wall — not breathing, not moving. Erma held out her hand and called, "George.... George... George." After a moment or two, he dropped his arms and fell back onto the bed in a seated position, still staring. There was deafening silence. No one moved. Finally, I realized what I had done.

Aunt Erma pointed with her finger to the door. It was absolutely clear that I had better get out of there immediately. She took the children into the living room and then returned to the kitchen with Uncle George. Neither my aunt or my uncle said anything to me that evening about the incident, about what I had done, or about Uncle George's reaction and his extreme state of duress.

In fact, nothing was said that night, or the next day, or ever. No one needed to. I learned many things that evening: a bit of insight as to what war can do to a soldier and how quickly those terrifying experiences can return. That a practical joke that may seem funny to one person can cause pain, hurt, and harm to another. I also learned a bit more about compassion, humility and controlling anger. Finally, I glimpsed the traumatic residua that can follow service to our country and the impact of guilt brought on by your own actions.

I Don't Know if it Happened This Way . . .

What I Will Miss

What I Will Miss Most...
When I sail away to that other shore,
Leaving behind me those I adore,
For the family and friends who remain,
Treasure moments like these that I will never experience again...

The warmth of Charlotte's body next to mine, as I wrap my arm around her soft warm glow, drift off to sleep, and in the morning, slowly awaken.

Watching our grandchildren maturing, finding love, entering their chosen careers, and perhaps someday, even having children of their own.

Celebrating the success and retirement of our children from their careers.

The wonderment and joy of celebrating holidays, birthdays, and special occasions together.

The smell of our well-searched Christmas tree in the house.

Charlotte's beautiful 'green thumb' flower gardens that bloom every year from early spring until the last leaves flutter down in late fall.

The joy of plucking a tomato, warmed by the sun, from the garden and enjoying the first bite as juice drips off my chin.

A slice of watermelon on a hot summer's day, so cold it almost hurts my teeth.

Dining together by candlelight using grandmother's best china, listening to Frank Patterson's wondrous voice singing the beautiful ballads of Ireland.

Enjoying fresh popcorn and a movie on the large screen and then discussing its meaning over a shared dessert in the café.

Lingering to listen to a music performance over a glass of wine.

All the wonderful smells: a newborn child, clean clothes, the air after a heavy rain, fall leaves, spring flowers, fudge on the stove, a wood fire in the dead of winter, a fresh baked pie, bread dough rising, an oven casserole, eggs and bacon at the campsite.

A mighty thunderstorm while safe and secure in one of our favorite places.

A road trip and exploring places we didn't know existed until we stumbled upon them.

A piece of warm pie that hasn't had a chance to cool with ice cream melting next to it on the dessert plate.

Fresh strawberry shortcake, hotdogs, and roasted corn on the cob.

Reading a good book, a glass of wine on the stand next to me, a fire in the fireplace, snow coming down, and the wind howling outside.

Climbing into bed at night and smelling the freshly laundered sheets that hung on the line outside all day.

Family and friends, near and far, that I will never see again.

What I Will Miss Most...
When I sail away to the other shore
Leaving friends and the family I adore
Please remember this: I shall miss
Every one of you across that deep abyss.

Perhaps We Just Reflect

What a year 2020 turned out to be, but it will end in a month as January 1st appears on the calendar. Personally, I cannot wait for the new year to arrive. It has been a year of memories, good ones, and others, maybe not so good. The not so good ones were highlighted by the COVID-19 virus and the ensuing isolation which it caused. We are still waiting out the pandemic as of this writing. Allow me to focus on one of my better memories I'm left this year.

On the Saturday before Thanksgiving, Charlotte and I were up at 5 a.m., getting dressed and ready for the opening day of deer season. Our son Todd was doing the same at his home as he planned on meeting us in Pultneyville where we would then drive out to the hunting area in two separate vehicles (still thinking about COVID-19 and distancing). The planning for this event began with us discussing his birthday present with him. Birthdays are important and celebrated in our family. As a part of this tradition, the birthday person is asked ahead of time for something they would really desire and appreciate as a gift. Todd's birthday was in early November and he thought a deer blind was the perfect gift. He said: "If Mom and Dad would go hunting with me this year. And by-the-way Mom, you could use the blind and be warm and comfortable in it."

Both Charlotte and I thought it would an enjoyable adventure to spend time together with our son, hunting. We did not focus on the fact that Charlotte had never hunted before. I had, but that had been more than sixty years ago. On the positive side, at different times in the past, both of us had already taken and completed the NYS hunter's safety course and we also have lifetime hunting and fishing licenses. I took the hunter safety course with my grandson when he was 14 years old as part of an agreement with his mother. I wanted to give him his first .22 rifle for a Christmas present and his mom agreed on the condition that he successfully complete the safety training course. Many years ago, a friend and work associate of Charlotte's, Kathy, wanted Charlotte to take the course with her so she could get her hunting license and be able to hunt with her husband but didn't want to take it alone. Kathy wanted to surprise her husband with the certificate she had earned. Both Charlotte and Kathy were successful in their quest. The course certificate is a requirement and is a big hurdle to be cleared before anyone can even think about getting a license and going into the woods to hunt, as it takes advance planning and a commitment of time (two weekends) before hunting season begins.

In preparation for our adventure, a decision had to be made as to what gun each of us would use. Charlotte made it clear to both Todd and me that she was not going with us until she had an opportunity to become familiar with the gun she was to use, practice firing it and target shooting with it. I have several rifles, and suggested to Todd that she might be comfortable with either the .357 or the .30-.30. Todd thought that perhaps she should use the 20 gauge shotgun.

Todd told me that he had my shotgun at his house as he had used it for the two previous deer seasons, but he only had two slugs left. He tried to buy more and had checked all the gun shops and sporting goods stores but there was no ammunition to be found anywhere, so he suggested, "I think Mom should use the .30-.30 and you can use the 20 gauge since it's yours and you're familiar with it."

With that decision agreed to, Charlotte and I were off to the Williamson Sportsman's Club gun range for little practice. I decided to take two of my rifles to the range, the .30-.30 and the .357. The .357 was a new gun that had never been fired, but both rifles are similar in their method of loading and firing so we would be doing basically the same things together at the range.

The .30-.30 is referred to as the '1894 model' and the rifle I have is an old, valuable collector's firearm. When we entered the range, another member was there and he was very interested in the gun Charlotte was carrying. He peppered her with a zillion questions about the gun. In passing, he looked at my rifle, asked what it was, I told him it was a Remington .357 and he responded, "I'm not interested in your gun, just your wife's Winchester, that's a nice deer rifle."

Charlotte and I each set up our separate targets at the distance of 50 yards. Together, we went over the loading, safety, and sighting of the rifles. We figured we would adjust the sights on hers after she fired the first five rounds. Since I had never fired the .357 before, I had no idea of how accurate it would be. Charlotte loaded five cartridges, and then took her time to sight and focus on the target, slowly squeezed the trigger, and fired. I did the same and fired at my target. We then walked out to the range to retrieve our targets and examine the results. I asked her if she wanted to shoot again and she elected to do so indicating that she enjoyed firing the rifle and it was, in her words, fun. No surprises here, as Charlotte had always enjoyed target shooting with me over the years. Later that evening, in my phone conversation with Todd, he asked how she did. I told him, "Mom fired ten rounds, and all her bullets hit the target, and each one of them was in the bull's eye."

As for me, the same could not be said. Todd and I talked about which gun we would each use and decided that Charlotte was fine with the Winchester .30-.30 and I should use the 20 gauge. I was very happy with the 20 gauge, as it was a gun I bought when I was just 16 years old. It was also the same gun I had used to shoot my first (and only) deer all those many years ago. I did not pursue deer hunting over the intervening years but that's a story for another time.

On Saturday, the opening day of the season, Charlotte was in the deer blind. I was a thousand feet away, in another field, sitting in the middle of walled-up stacks of firewood. Todd was further and deeper into the woods, out back near the swamp. It was just beginning to turn from darkness to daylight as the sun was rising, but still too early to shoot, as it was before the 7 a.m. starting time. Sitting silently and alert, listening to the sounds of the woods; I noticed the birds chirping their welcoming morning songs, the geese flying above in formation and honking encouragement to their leaders, an owl hooting off in the distance as if announcing morning had arrived, and some small unseen little creature rustling in the leaves and in the woodpile behind me.

My mind wandered as I thought about the differences in these woods and the woods I was sitting in six decades ago... My spouse is here sharing this same experience with me, as is our son. He was not even a thought in my consciousness or reality all those many years ago. Yes, it is a better time. A time to be cherished, held close, to be inhaled, to be loved. The world turns on its axis, time stops for no one and continues to 'tick' on, ever unrelenting, as both time and life marches on, hand in hand. It was the perfect day! How do we hold on to these thoughts and memories, both then and now, and how do we share these with others we care so much about? It is not important whether we go home with a deer this morning, this afternoon, or even this season. Perhaps we shouldn't? Perhaps all we really need to do is just reflect on the day and the experience. Perhaps...

1940 and Today

I was born in 1940, on August 8th, to be exact. The calendar indicates it was on Thursday. The major news stories and headlines of the time included that the Luftwaffe began its Blitz on London, Japan launched the Yamato, which was the biggest battleship ever to set sail, Germany and Italy controlled most of Western Europe. Meanwhile, here in the US; race riots were taking place in Chicago, Harlem, Los Angeles and Detroit, Gone with the Wind was a newly released movie and it was a hit, jazz was the popular music of the day being played by Benny Goodman, Count Basie, and many others, nylon stockings were just being introduced to the market, FDR was elected for a third term, the country was starting to emerge from the Great Depression, and factory workers were able to earn up to $1,250 a year.

My family was firmly anchored in the lower middle class at best. I was a male, and by today's definitions, could have been, I suppose, classified as being of white privilege, or societal privilege that benefits white people over nonwhite people in some societies, particularly if they are otherwise under the same social, political, or economic circumstances. I was offered educational opportunities for thirteen years while attending public schools followed by an opportunity to attend college which I am ashamed to admit, I did not take full advantage of until a few years later in my life. It took a while for me to realize the importance of a solid, well-rounded education. I was blessed with an internal yearning and drive to achieve, which combined with pure unadulterated good luck, the aid of great mentors and friends, hard work, blessed to have found love and a lifetime partner, had a family, and have enjoyed good health, prosperity, and long life... so far, so good.

Now questions come to the forefront of my mind and thoughts in those quiet hours of reflection. Questions regarding white privilege and the role fate may have played in my life and how of any of the following would have impacted me and who I turned out to be.

- ✓ Was it being born a male?
- ✓ Was it white privilege?
- ✓ Was it a college education?
- ✓ Was it the class I was born into?
- ✓ Was it my parents?
- ✓ Was it how I was raised?
- ✓ Was it good health?
- ✓ Was it work experiences at General Motors, Kodak, school districts, and universities?
- ✓ Was it a college degree?
- ✓ Was it the advanced degrees?
- ✓ Was it that I was married?
- ✓ Was it that I had a family?
- ✓ Was it that I was too young to have served in a war with Korea?
- ✓ Was it that I was married and had children when the draft was instituted for Vietnam?

I think often of these questions and ponder possible answers, outcomes, and how the stars were aligned in the heavens when the forks in the road appeared. I also think about the role that pure dumb chance or luck may have played. What other opportunities or options were there, of lack thereof, made all the difference?

What would have happened at the very moment of conception if the combination of chromosomes would have been XX rather than XY?

What would have been different had I been born in a foreign country?

What would have happened had I been born Brown, Black, Asian, or some combination of all the possibilities that exist?

What would have been different if I didn't have a college degree?

What would have happened if I never found true love or married or had a family?

What would have been my fate if I was forced to go to war?

What would have been my fate if I were born into true poverty or into wealth?

What is luck or fate?

What control do we have over who we are or are to become?

If I were not me, who would I be?

Consider the possibilities; be thankful, be kind, be humble, live every day to the fullest, create opportunities for others, leave the world a better place than the way you found it, love others, and be true to who you are and were meant to be.

I Don't Know if it Happened This Way . . .

Can You See the Other Side of the Moon?

I had a dream the other night. The location was Jefferson High School. I was teaching my earth science class, woke up, and the scary part was that the students were sitting there laughing at me. The lesson was to demonstrate for the class that here on earth, we can only see one side of the moon, or what we call the face of the moon, when we look up at night. The emphasis was placed on the fact that no human, over the centuries, has ever seen the back or the other side of the moon from earth. Our textbook even stated this very fact, and it was left to me to explain it to them. I knew this was an important tidbit since it had appeared in question form on a few past year-end Regents exams. I had to make this point and explain or demonstrate it for them.

I had a student stand in the center of the room and had another student walk around the perimeter of the room, always looking at and facing his classmate standing in the center while she kept looking at his face. After one trip around the room, I asked the student in the center if she ever saw the back of the head of the person walking around the room. The answer was, "No." My question to the class was, "Why?"

After much discussion, more questions, and repeating the demonstration a few times, the class realized that synchronous rotation was being demonstrated. That is, the student walking around the outside of the room had made one 360-degree turn or revolution in his or her body. In the same amount of time, he or she never showed the back of his or her head. The student in the center had also made one 360-degree turn of his or her body, or one revolution. Both students had made one complete revolution on their journey in the demonstration. Before the bell rang, everyone wanted to roleplay and interchange the two positions of the demonstration and so they did. I'm certain they left class with an understanding of synchronous rotation of the earth and the moon.

In my dream, when the bell rang, I glanced at my planning calendar on the desk and noticed it was opened to January 17, 2021. That's when I woke up, realizing everyone was laughing at me. My dream was "dated" based on the actual timeline of my experience, which was1966, years before the Apollo mission and the landing on the moon. The students and everyone else in the world had seen firsthand on television or on reruns the entire moon's surface from the images taken from the Command Module, Columbia. Their teacher is now telling them, no one has ever seen the other side or back side of the moon. They knew the Eagle had landed in the Sea of Tranquility, more than 50 years ago.

I guess I need to update my lesson plans for next year or think of retiring before I dream on!

Contemplate

I hold in my hands a piece of history that could have been created thousands of years ago. It has the potential of being recreated or recycled hundreds of times since it was found on a mountain or buried deep underground, dug up, carted to, and placed in a blast furnace. I am about to recreate the piece once again, not in a furnace, but with tools, heat, and a welding process. This piece is dense, heavy, and feels cool to the touch. Depending on how it is treated, it can be smooth and reflective as a glass mirror or rough, scaly, round, flat, broad, thin, or razor sharp.

It has been known and used by mankind for over 4,000 years, and since it can be repurposed and reprocessed, it retains its properties because of its ability to "bounce back" to its original shape after being deformed under stress. I will rework it once again and stress it once more. In a previous life this very piece I'm holding in my hands could have been part of the rails that crossed our country in the 1800s, or the locomotive running on the tracks, a paddle wheeler cruising down the Mississippi, a sewing machine your great grandmother used, an Army tank from one of those great wars, a 1918 Ford model T, my old, but once new, 1965 Chevrolet, or my neighbor's old kitchen appliance before it was recycled and arrived at my workshop.

Let Mother Nature have her way with this, and with years on her side, time could well change it to any of colors ranging from caramel to coffee, cedar, cinnamon, chocolate, umber, walnut, pecan, hickory, carob, mocha, or any of the other various shades of brown. Scientists and chemists have a simple explanation for this color change. Its reddish-brown color is a form of iron oxide due to exposure to an oxygen rich environment. I simply call it rust. The beauty of this mocha-colored piece of history I'm holding is that it can be reworked and changed, depending on how I handle and treat it. I can transform it into a smooth and reflective mirror-like finish once again or another shape of my choosing. I'm the one in charge and will determine its fate, shape, color, purpose, use, style, application, and future destiny for a period of time from a day or two or a century. It just depends...

This piece of steel "speaks" to me as I contemplate its recreation. Could it be a bowl, lamp, dancer, gate, table, desk, chime, bell, or take on some abstract form? What is the vision, color, form, finish, size, purpose, application, and will it find a new home? It can be hammered, welded, bent, heated, twisted, smoothed, polished, acid treated, or left to the whims of Mother Nature. As time marches on, this beautiful (in my mind) art piece, could once again become a weapon, kitchen appliance, new automobile, or Army tank. For after all, it is not permanent, it can be repurposed and reworked. Oh, that I could say the same for myself.

The Penguin and the Cardboard Box Caper

The genesis and background for this tale was created in 1941 by Bob Kane and Bill Finger in DC Comics. This occurred early in Batman's comic career as other characters were being developed and introduced to the readers. The Penguin is one of Batman's most enduring enemies and is among the group of collective adversaries the makes up Batman's rogues gallery. The Penguin is always after power, on the side of 'good' and wants the city of Gotham to be peaceful and prosperous. When the rotund Penguin waddled into the 1941 comic panel scene, the setting was an art show. Later that same evening, two famous paintings came up missing, and after the show was over, the Penguin connected with a member of the local mob in Gotham for the purpose of selling the paintings. When one of the mob members asked another, "What's his name?" he was told simply to call him, "the Penguin."

In the following connected tale, there was no art show, but there happened to be a faculty meeting. The Rochester City School District had decided to reorganize all the Junior and Senior High Schools. The Senior High School, where I had been teaching for three years, was being converted to a Jr.-Sr. High School, which meant that classrooms had to be relocated. Some teachers were being transferred to new room assignments, while others were being transferred to different schools within the district to balance enrollments and class size. All of this meant a massive packing, moving, and unpacking initiative of the individual teacher's personal and classroom materials, supplies, and books over the summer months while teachers were on vacation. After the packing was scheduled to be completed by teachers, the actual moving of the materials was to be accomplished by various custodial and central warehouse staff utilizing City trucks. One can just imagine the complexity and logistics involved in this massive move within the buildings in the district.

Teachers and staff members were notified that they had to attend a special, and extended time, faculty meeting on a Wednesday in early June of that same year. It was made crystal clear that attendance was mandatory, as moving and packing instructions were to be reviewed for faculty in order to prepare our rooms for the reorganization. Booklets were printed and distributed at the start of the meeting which included schedules, dates, and timelines. As teachers, our responsibilities for packing, unpacking, and setting up our new rooms were detailed and outlined. At about this point in the faculty meeting things began to get a bit silly from the staffs' viewpoint.

The meeting was being run by our Vice Principle who was a dear man. He was a lifelong bachelor who did not drive but he rode the city bus to and from school every day. School was his life. He was rather short, a bit rotund, and he was always prepared for inclement weather with rubbers on his shoes and an umbrella with a curved handle, which he carried hanging over his left arm while carrying a large attaché case and his bag lunch in the other. In the winter, he always wore a heavy woolen overcoat, fur covered hat, and oversized rubber boots on his shoes, which had buckles that snapped together all the way up the front. And the dear old man's feet did not point straight ahead in the direction in which he was going, but rather they were angled to the right and left of the directional straight line he was headed, and he waddled a bit as he meandered. When he walked, he waddled a bit from side to side, reminding the observer of watching penguins move towards the pool of water at the zoo. His wire-rimmed glasses completed his nerdy but scholarly appearance. As a group of young teachers, we had given our VP a nickname taken directly from our childhood and the DC comics, "The Penguin."

About 40 minutes into the meeting, the VP (Mr. V.) decided to show us the correct way to assemble a shipping box, pack, label, and seal it. This process consumed about 30 minutes of the meeting, first by starting with a flat box obtained from the district's central warehouse. Mr. V. began the demonstration by unfolding it, then folding in the end flaps, folding the bottom, turning the box over, demonstrating the proper length of tape to use, how to attach the tape to the side before covering the bottom flaps, then continuing up the opposite side of the box, cutting the tape and securing the end on the side flap. Next, he demonstrated the correct way to fill out the label before attaching it to the box. A form was projected on the screen, "This is where you place your name, list your current room number, the name of school, your new room number assignment from the booklet, the name of the new school, if being transferred, and a complete list the contents you are placing in this box. Be specific!" Mr. V. continued to demonstrate how to pack by actually filling the box.

It was at this moment that my buddy, the graphic arts teacher, Jeff Hulme, leaned over to me and said, "I can't take any more of this box crap, and I don't believe The Penguin even knows what a box is. Want to have some fun? What are you doing tonight if we ever get out of this effin' meeting?"

Finally, at about 4:45 p.m. we were all released from purgatory. As you can imagine, there were a lot of negative comments and unhappy people trying to get out of the room all at the same moment. Jeff grabbed my arm and we walked towards the parking lot. "Got some time to have some fun?" "Sure," I responded. That afternoon we made three trips to grocery stores, picking up as many empty cardboard boxes that we could cram into the back of Jeff's truck. Each time we drove back to Jefferson High and into the bay of the auto shop, we unloaded all the boxes and carried them to the main office. We made up a story and talked the night custodian into letting us into the main office and unlocking the door to the Penguin's office. By 7:00 p.m. we had boxes stuffed into every corner and empty space of the office and up to the very ceiling, around the fluorescent lights, on the chairs and desk, and the last thing we did was to push and hold the boxes into the room so we could get the door closed. When we were finished, we asked the custodian if he would please lock Mr. V's and the main office door for us.

We knew Mr. V's daily schedule as well as he did, so Jeff and I were checking our mailboxes earlier than usual the next morning at 7:00 a.m., when Mr. V. arrived and we quietly watched as he slid his key into the lock of the door, and as he turned it, pushing hard on the door to get it open, we watched the mountain of boxes cascade out of the door into the lobby. Jeff and I tried to stifle our laughs and quickly exited, out the side door, down the hall, with Mr. V. in hot pursuit. Jeff and I were at least 50 feet away and about to turn the corner of the main hall when we heard, "Buehler, you're fired. Hulme, you're fired too! Stop where you are!" Mr. V. caught up with us and bellowed, "I want to see you both in my office in ten minutes."

Ten minutes later we were both seated on the bench next to the mailboxes and opposite his office door. Ironically, this was the very same bench that students had to sit on when sent to the office for disciplinary referrals awaiting a meeting with the VP. Mr. V. approached both of us, a bit red in the face, sputtering "You know I can't fire you because of the union contract, but if I could... I would!"

Both Jeff and I signed up for the district's and union's offer of a voluntary transfer to a new school for the next school year. When I stopped in the office on the last day of school to drop off my sign-out sheet and pick up my last paycheck, Mr. V. wished me good luck. I apologized and told him I was sorry for stuffing his office full of empty boxes. He responded with an ever so slight smile and a comment, "Funny and clever, but next time you have an idea for a joke, think carefully and thoughtfully before you act."

All was well in Gotham City the last day of school that year; "The Penguin" wanted the city to be peaceful and prosperous.

I Don't Know if it Happened This Way . . .

Red Shirt and His Drums

As a family tradition, we have sent out a Christmas letter rather than a commercial card for the holidays. For decades, one such mailing was addressed to:

> Red Shirt
> Taos Pueblo
> Taos New Mexico, 87580

Why just Red Shirt and no other name or names? Strange, I know. Most Hopis do not celebrate the holidays. But nevertheless, every year, the same address was handwritten on one of our Christmas letters for mailing. Each one had a return address affixed and not one mailing had ever been returned, so my assumption was that Red Shirt had received them.

Our connection with Red Shirt began when our family was on an extended vacation on a six-week trip across the country focusing on the western states, National Parks, and all interesting points in-between, but making a conscious effort to try to avoid traditional tourist sites, gift shops, and roadside attractions. There were five of us in the family, with Todd being the youngest and he was still a few years shy of becoming a teenager. He is 52 now so you can calculate how many years ago this tale took place, for after all, the author is under no obligation to answer any questions you may have about Red Shirt at this juncture in this tale.

Our journey was planned so that we could visit many of the Hopi reservations and pueblos of the Southwest including the Taos Pueblo.

Todd had his heart set on buying a handcrafted drum to take home to remind him of the trip and of course, to play with it. Outside of Taos, we stumbled upon an establishment that sold drums to the public and stopped and shopped, looking for the perfect drum. Todd, as well as Mom and Dad, were very interested in acquiring an authentic handmade drum by a Native American. We all asked many questions about the drums we found interesting, but the answers we received left us with many blanks to be filled in. In our discussions, we discovered that there was a well-known native drum maker who lived in the Taos Pueblo and that some of his drums were at the establishment we had shopped at. We asked for and were shown a couple of examples of his drums. We were intrigued with each of them.

Back in the car, I suggested something to the effect of, "Todd, wouldn't it be nice to buy your drum directly from the person who made it rather than from a store?" Todd was excited and 'all in' on this idea while his sisters were a bit embarrassed and raised questions about how we were to find the person, get into the pueblo, find his home, and then, ask to buy one of his drums? We had gotten his name from the clerk at the store who had shown us his drums. The drum maker was Red Shirt, and we knew, from the clerk, that he had a home in the 1,000-year-old Pueblo in Taos. We drove to the Pueblo and started inquiring of folks if they knew a person by the name Red Shirt and if perchance, where he lived. The answers came quick and easy. I drove down a dirt road to where I was told he lived, parked out front, got out and knocked on the door. The girls stayed in the car and looked like they were about to die of embarrassment. A gentleman opened the door, and I explained I was looking for Red Shirt, the drum maker for the village, and that it would indeed be an honor, if possible, to meet him.

"I'm Red Shirt, please come in and invite everyone in the car to come in if you wish."

Our daughters were now totally embarrassed by their dad who, with no shame and with any hesitation, drove up in front of the home, got out and went to the door and knocked. Red Shirt explained the details of drum making and showed us his workshop. He took us out to the courtyard to show us the hollowed out cottonwood tree trunks used for the drums, deer and elk hides, and told us how the hides were cured and tanned in urine, how he laced the drum head, and crafted the drumsticks and raw hide cover and wrapping. We then went back into his home and he let Todd pick out any drum he wanted. We were delighted and Todd now had his treasured drum. During the afternoon visit and interactions, we learned that Red Shirts' daughter was living in NYC but he and his wife had never been out of Taos and they were planning to drive to NYC for their daughter's wedding, which had been planned for the week after the Labor Day weekend. We chatted a bit more and discussed the trip, route, and their plans. We suggested that since they were driving and had planned to drive on Route 90 through New York that they may wish to stay with us at our home and rest a day or two before driving on to the city. They indicated that they would like to do so and we wrote down our home and work phone numbers as well as our address and told him we looked forward to having him and his wife spend Labor Day weekend with us.

"Just call us when you are close, and we'll meet you and you can follow us to our home."

Labor Day came and went, the school year started, and we never heard a word or received a phone call from Red Shirt. A few more weeks passed and the end of September was rapidly approaching. One day, I was in class and a student appeared at the door with a note from the main office that there was a person waiting on the phone wishing to speak with me.

"Hello Gary, this is Red Shirt."

"Hi, we were wondering where you were. Are you in New York or near Rochester?"

"Yes."

"Where are you?"

"We are not sure where we are, but we saw a sign that read Zoo and we followed it and we are in a parking lot."

"Red Shirt, are you in a parking at the Zoo?"

"Yes."

"Stay right where you are. My school ends in about a half-hour and I'll be right over. It will take me about another half-hour to drive there so I'll see you around 4:30."

I called my wife to let her know Red Shirt and his wife were in town, that he just called me at school, and he and his wife would be having dinner with us and staying for the night. She wanted to know for how long would they be staying and what we should we plan to have for dinner? I told her I have no idea of how long they would be staying or why they didn't come on Labor Day weekend as planned, but how about we have an old-fashioned summer picnic dinner that night?

As I pulled into the parking lot at the Zoo, I'm wondering what kind of a car I should be looking for and was a bit upset with myself that

I was so flustered I forgot to ask him that question earlier. Immediately, I realized there was no need for me to fret or worry. As I pulled into the parking lot, I glanced around and spotted an old Chevy pickup truck, and there, on the hood, sitting on a blanket, leaning back against the windshield, was Red Shirt and his wife, looking totally relaxed. I drove up to the truck and greeted them both and suggested they follow me home. We were delighted and excited to see each other. They were a long way from home.

That evening, we had red and white hot dogs, potato salad, corn on the cob, and watermelon for dessert. The white hot dogs were something new for them, as was steamed corn. With regards to corn on the cob, our family enjoyed it as usual, but I did notice that the platter of corn passed by our guests twice with neither helping themselves to an ear.

"Red Shirt, I'm wondering if you don't care for corn?"

"I'm sorry, we don't know how we should eat it. It's on the cob and when it's on the cob, we feed it to our animals. How do you eat it on the cob?"

"Try taking one, put a lot of butter on it like this, and if you like salt and pepper, add that, hold it like this, and bite along the rows."

It was a hit and a first-time experience for them, as were the interstate highways, the cities, towns, and the Zoo, and I'm sure, our lifestyle and perhaps our cultural practices, food, and living arrangements.

"Gary, why does the city keep all those animals in pens, behind bars, on concrete, and in the Zoo?"

I was l at a loss for words to try to answer his inquiry that would make any sense to him and to me after all the animal life we saw in the wild and enjoyed on our summer trip. His probing question was to help him to try to understand how we, as folks here in the East, could appreciate these beautiful creatures when they are not free to roam. Great question!

That evening we drove down to Charlotte Beach and Durand to show them the shore of Lake Ontario. They stood silently, mesmerized, without moving for a very long time, looking out across the water to the horizon. The sun was beginning to set in the West.

"Gary, so much water. We have never seen this much water. We must carry buckets of water from the creek to our corn plants every day so that they will grow. No one at the Pueblo will believe me when I tell them what you have here and what I've seen."

Our guests stayed the rest of the week and it was a wonderful experience for all. They enjoyed our family and our kids enjoyed them and asked hundreds of questions about native life, living, beliefs, customs, practices, school, hunting, farming, etc. The questions were endless and wonderful understanding and learning took place. We figured out that, at least for Red Shirt and his wife, time, dates, and calendars are not priorities in their life. Time, for them, has a much different meaning. We learned that they had spoken to their daughter by phone and let her know they would visit her after her wedding as they had been invited to a major Native American powwow being held in Niagara Falls, and after that event, they would drove on to NYC. We learned that Red Shirt had many of his drums in the truck to sell at the public part of the event and his wife, who was a potter, also had pots to sell. They were both hoping to finance their trip with their sales. The visit ended with our guests inviting us to join them at the powwow on Sunday evening, after the event concluded and was then closed to the public. Red Shirt explained that this was a religious event for him and his fellow Native Americans and we would be attending as his guests. He advised us to refrain from taking photos and stay in the background, and assured us that there would be no problems with our attending as we were his invited guests.

On that very special Sunday evening, we were we just one of a few of the non-native attendees and for everyone in our family, it was a new experience to hear and view the singing, dancing, and the playing of the drums. Before our guests left our home on Saturday morning, Red Shirt's wife gifted each one of us with one of her pottery pieces she had created and I'm pretty certain had planned to sell at the exhibit that weekend. Those pieces are still with us as well as the memories they evoke. And as for Todd's drum, it resides with him at his home, and Red Shirts' other drum, the one that was a gift when he stayed with us all those years ago, I'm looking at it now, on the bookshelf in our family room.

Many years have passed since our family visited with Red Shirt at the Pueblo and dozens of annual Christmas letters and greetings have been mailed to him. We have made numerous trips over the years to the Southwest. On one of our most recent trips, we passed through Taos and I suggested to Charlotte that we stop and say, "Hello" to Red Shirt. I remembered where he lived and how to get there. We were able to drive up to and stop in front of his home. I parked, got out, walked up to the door and knocked, as I did so many years ago. Everything appeared the same as it was in my memory. A woman answered the door and opened it.

"Hi, I'm Gary. I was here years ago with my family and we have two of Red Shirt's drums."

It was so obvious that I'd caught her off guard. The look on her face told me that something was amiss...

"Why don't you come around to the side door?" She offered.

As I walked through the outdoor patio, I noticed there were no drums hanging in the windows or any in the workshop as we entered that room. All the cotton wood tree trunks were gone, as were the hides waiting to be cut into drumheads.

"I know who you are. You are the man who sent my father a Christmas letter every year! Red Shirt was my father. He died two years ago. I'm so sorry he's not here to welcome you. He always looked forward to your letter every year. We have different religious beliefs and that is why he never sent Christmas cards to you. I received your letter this year, addressed to Red Shirt. Thank you. I wish my father were here to visit with you."

As I watched the Pueblo slowly fading from view in the mirror as we drove away, I thought I could hear, ever so faintly, the rhythmic beating of the powwow communal drum, singing, and chanting of prayers. It was a special moment and memory to recall.

The Cat, Parakeet, and Fruit Cake

The door was locked and no one had opened it or entered for a week. The key slid easily into the lock, and with an audible click, and with a turn of the doorknob, I slowly pushed the door open. My spouse was my shadow and replicated my every move as I stepped into the room. With a quick glance around both the living and dining rooms, my eyes stopped and froze on our parakeet cage in the corner by the bookshelf.

The once ever-so-beautiful bird of every shade of blue was sitting motionless, perched on her swing in the center of her cage and her universe. She no longer sang her amorous song with sharp tweets accompanied by her head bobbing and head feathers erect letting us know, "I'm here!" All was deadly silent from the cage, not even a squawk.

Slowly approaching the cage, the first thing we noticed was our darling parakeet was missing every single tail feather. Staring blankly into the cage, we noticed her tail feathers were all in the bottom of her cage with a few that had fallen out and were on the floor below. "Where's the cat?" was my response.

We searched the bedrooms first, then the bathroom, followed by the kitchen, and we were standing in the middle of the living room when we noticed the cat perched on the top of the drapes of the front picture window. I went to grab her and take her down and she hissed, growled, showed her fangs, and I swear to you, actually spat at me. I stood on the sofa, reached up to grab her and she went crazy, running across the top of the drapes, down the other side and into the bedroom, up those drapes and across the top to the far end. We noticed all the drapes and curtains in every room were ripped and torn. I had to figure out what I was going to do with the cat, who was now acting bat-s___ crazy and was now an attack animal. If I was lucky enough to catch her, what in the world was I going to do with her?

Wandering back into the kitchen, both of us were staring at a rainbow of colors cascading down the door and the front of the refrigerator. The colors seemed to be flowing down from the multi-colored pool on the top of the appliance located just under the cake platter. The rum cake sitting on the platter had apparently fermented during the past week having benefited from the warm environment of the kitchen and the fact that the thermostat had been set at 70 degrees waiting for our return. First things first... my spouse proceeded to clean up the cake mess and assigned me to take care of the cat. I called my uncle George and asked him if he wouldn't mind having another barn cat on the farm. I was now, more than ever, willing to donate and deliver this loco cat even if it was a five-hour round trip drive. I had decided the next trip for that cat was going to be to my uncle's farm in Cameron, NY. My only real concern and challenge was not the cat, but how was I going to explain all of this to our two girls without breaking their hearts?

How did all of this happen? We need to turn the calendar back one week prior to entering the apartment. We had made plans to attend a party and drop our two girls off at my mother's for her to babysit them. After stopping at Grandma's for our daughters to spend the evening with her, we went on to enjoy the party. That evening the weather turned nasty. We left our friend's house around midnight and headed to Grandma's, planning to stay the night since the weather was so poor, then head home the next morning which was Sunday. On the way to Grandma's, driving north, with the wind blowing from the west, big fluffy flakes were coming down, making visibility difficult and the roads nearly impassable. It was a true lake-effect snowstorm, a real blizzard. The wind was causing snow drifts in the road that were difficult if not impossible to drive through. We finally did reach my grandma's home in Greece well after midnight. It was early morning, so we decided to stay the night and go to our apartment the next morning.

Upon arising at my mom's house, we were surprised to see the wind still blowing hard, causing huge drifts in the driveway and in the street out in front of the house. We were in the middle of a blizzard and the radio and TV news were predicting continuing high winds, many more inches of snow for the day, continuing through the evening and into the next day. Eventually, January 29 and 30, 1966 was to go down in the weather history book for Rochester, NY as the Blizzard of '66. When the blizzard finally ended, a total accumulation of almost 30" of snow was recorded along with notations that 30-foot snow drifts had developed at locations near Lake Ontario, paralyzing the city and the area, shutting down the city and suburbs for nearly a week. Wholesale food suppliers, outlets, homes and the community were running out of food. Emergency vehicles and snowplows were snow bound and couldn't get through the drifts.

We woke up to all of this Sunday morning at my mother's house. At the time I was a non-traditional college student, that is, I was married and was a full-time college student in my senior year and employed full-time at General Motors in Rochester. We had a one-year-old car, fully paid for, and I had planned to finish my senior year and graduate in May. I was anxious to attend classes on Monday and not miss any time from work. Sunday morning, the snow continued and each hour it just kept accumulating, blowing, and drifting.

After three hours, I had shoveled my car out of the drifts in the driveway and had cleared enough snow that I thought I could make it out to the street. My uncle Paul stopped at Mom's house after I called him and asked him to bring over a set of tire chains for my car. He worked part time at a Gulf gas station on Lyell Avenue and we decided that we could get to the station and put the chains on in the warm garage so that I could drive back to my mom's house and then back to our apartment and I'd be all set for school and work the next day. I had no clue as to how much snow had accumulated and that the road crews and plows were unable to handle clearing the roadways.

Paul and I, feeling fearless and invincible, headed out, taking the only routes possible, which were north-south roads, knowing we would encounter huge snow drifts. We were on Manitou Road and visibility was almost zero from the blowing snow. About two miles south of Ridge Road our luck ran out.

With the side windows down a bit, and with Paul judging where we were in the road by trying to keep his eye on the telephone poles on his side of the road and with me trying to keep my eyes on the mail boxes on my side, we plowed into a drift that buried us and we were unable to go any further. Paul jumped out and ran up to a house that had the porch light on, to ask to use their phone. He arrived back to the car informing me that he had called a tow truck and it was on its way to assist us.

We keep the engine running, the heat on, and constantly cleared the heavy snow off the windshield and back window to see if we could spot any vehicles coming and that were on the road. A half hour or so later, I noticed flashing yellow lights in my rear-view mirror, excitedly hollered that the tow truck was coming, and we both jumped out of the car. The tow truck driver did not see us or my car and drove right into the back of it. Paul was waving his arms and yelling, "Stop!" and at the last second he realized the driver didn't see us or the car due to blizzard conditions. Paul turned and started to run, just a split second too late as the wooden front bumper of the truck caught him in the buttocks, sending him flying. I was in the road and missed being struck. Thank goodness Paul picked himself up after his short flight and we climbed back into the car to try to warm up a bit.

The truck driver called the Greece Police on his radio and 15 minutes or so later we saw the flashing red lights moving towards us slowly. The policeman arrived, spoke with the driver, collected the information he needed for the accident report and sent him on his way to his next call. The policeman also took down my information for his report from the front seat of his patrol car and told me he would call another tow truck for me.

We both waited until we saw flashing yellow lights coming from the other direction. Yes, it happened AGAIN! Due to the wind, the whiteout, the drifts, and the blizzard, the second tow truck didn't see my car in the drift either, nor the flashing red lights of the police car behind my car and drove right into the front of my car. When this happened all three of us, the policeman, Paul, and I were standing in the road. The police took the second driver's information for his report, supervised the driver hooking up my car to be towed away, and then he drove Paul and I back to my mother's house. By the time we arrived at Mom's, Paul was sore and barely able to walk, and his behind was already black and blue. The next day, it even looked worse and he was very sore.

By the week's end, some of the roads had been cleared and were barely passible. Travel was restricted. Uncle Paul drove us home to our apartment in the city, and you now know the rest of the story (the cat, the parakeet, and the rum cake). A few weeks later, my almost new '65 Chevy had been repaired, fenders and bumpers replaced, and newly painted. The cat never did adjust to being a farm cat.

I did inquire about the kitty and Uncle George told me, "That dam cat you brought down here jumped on my head, dug her claws into my scalp when I tried taking her to the barn, that was one crazy cat!" When I heard the past tense being used, I knew better than to inquire any further. As for the parakeet, she didn't make it through to the end of the week, having fallen off her perch and we found her in the bottom of her cage, looking ever so sad without her tail feathers. We had bird funeral for the girls and for us.

The official weather bureau's recording of the snowfall for the blizzard of 1966 was 28.8" on January 30 and 31. General Motors and school were closed for the week so I didn't miss anything. We still tell the story of Uncle Paul flying through the air. We never had another parakeet but did have a new kitty that was gentle and sane.

The Wedding

It should never have happened. It might have just been easier to say "No." It always amazes me how things turn out when crazy ideas burst forth in bright sunlight. Take for example, a conversation I had with an elementary principal twenty-seven years ago.

BP   "You know that Jim and I are engaged and in the middle of planning our wedding, but things are rapidly changing. Since our wedding announcement and photo appeared in the newspaper months ago, my students and parents know that next month we are going to be married on the third Saturday. We're not sure how to handle all the requests we are receiving. Several parents and students have made appointments and stopped in to see me and want to know if they can attend the ceremony. I really don't know how to say no to their requests without hurting feelings and burning bridges. Several of the parents that are asking if they can attend and bring their elementary school child with them are also members of our school's PTA. We previously sent invitations to a select few staff and faculty members. I don't know where to draw the line now we've done that and tell others they are not invited."

Me   "Have you thought about responding by saying, "We have planned this for adults only, no children?"

BP   "We have. Some of the staff, faculty, and parents are also members of the church where we made plans to be married so I am certain they are going to be there. We really don't mind children attending. How can we say yes to a few and no to others? We just don't know how to limit all the elementary school students and parents who want to attend."

Me   "Ohhh, Lauren, I see the challenge."

BP   "That's why I wanted to talk with you. Jim and I have been talking together about perhaps changing our plans. If we open the wedding up to the whole school community, there will not be enough room in the church. So, we have been thinking about having our wedding in the school and have an open invitation to everyone who may wish to attend. We have discussed this idea with the minister, and he is fine with the wedding being held in the school. What do you think? Would this be possible?"

Me   "Well.... I'm thinking... legalities, Board of Education approval, school facilities usage regulations, and when word gets out, and it will, I'm thinking TV news stations and cameras, newspaper reporters, and what happens with the next wedding request that the district may receive."

BP   "Jim and I think the elementary students would love to be a part of our wedding. They have been chatting about it for weeks. Would you mind seeing if you can get approval?"

I just realized what happened. Lauren walked in to chat with me with a monkey on her back. When she left, the monkey was now on my back. A wise administer should not allow this to occur. So much for being wise...

This was a small town and tight community that supported its schools and I happen to be a calculated risk-taker with a big heart. The easy answer to the Lauren's question would have been to flatly and simply said "No," but I choose a different route. The school attorney didn't find anything in the district's regulations or education law that would block the request. To be honest here, I requested that he not dig too deep or look too hard as I did not want him to find anything to block the request. I discussed the situation with the Board, and suggested it would work out fine, and they unanimously approved. And so it came to pass that Mr. and Mrs. James and Lauren Shuman were married in the West Side Elementary School on the third Saturday the following month amid laughter, applause, and tears of joy. The atmosphere at the school the day of the ceremony was like a Disney fairy tale wedding and each one of them felt that they were an intricate and important part of the wedding. A video clip of the married couple leaving through the front doors of the school after the ceremony played on the 6:00 and 11:00 o'clock TV news broadcasts.

It was rumored that the grocery store sold out all its bags and boxes of rice early that same Saturday morning. This was the one and only wedding in any of the four schools in the Gouverneur School District during the past twenty-seven years. How could one say no? Sometimes when one takes a calculated risk, one gets lucky, or at the very least, somewhere a guardian angel is keeping watch over the flock, the foolish, the brave, and perhaps, just perhaps, the unwise.

A Horse By Any Other Name...

Harold explained it all to me and I believed him. "It's easy.... all horses like apples, and they'll come to you when you hold an apple in your hand." I wanted to ride this beauty named Babe but she wanted nothing to do with me. When I'd walk down to the fence at the edge of the pasture, she'd eye me carefully and when I got too close, she'd gallop away down the cow path towards the bank that formed the dam on one end of the pond.

Babe was a very spirited, although older, retired rodeo pony whose life was spent assisting her rider in roping calves. Due to her animated reactions and her free spirt, she was injured in an accident when she ran out of her former owner's stable trying to get away. She ran right into a horizontal pipe and it pierced her head just below her eye. She never fully recovered from the injury and her owner grew impatient applying salve and ointment to the wound daily and waiting for the wound to heal. He put her out for adoption as he could no longer deal with the nursing responsibilities.

My Uncle George loved animals and tried to save everyone, especially when the price was right. In Babe's case, the price was a freebee. I was there the day the truck backed down the drive way to the barn and delivered her to the farm. I could see how upset and agitated Babe was as she was moving around and hitting the side racks of the truck bed. The minute the gate to the pasture was opened and the gate of the truck was unlatched, and before the ramp was pulled out and lowered, Babe's hooves never touched the ramp as she jumped out of the truck and ran like the wind down the cow path to the lower pasture. The owner turned to my uncle and said something like:

"Good luck, I don't think you'll ever get a bridle over her head, a bit in her mouth, or a blanket and saddle on her back. I'd suggest you never try to ride her. She's too wild and rambunctious to be tamed and ridden again. She was a good and fast roping pony and never wanted to let a calf get away from her, backing up, keeping the rope taut... but I'm afraid those days are gone. Since her accident, she hasn't been the same."

I took two apples from the basket in the back room of the porch just off the kitchen. My three cousins were playing outside and they wanted to know what the apples were for and where I was going. I told them I wanted ride on Babe in the pasture. They wanted to know if they could go with me and if they could ride also. I told them to go and get their own apples. We were marching to the barn like some kind of parade and were excited that each one of us was anticipating our own "roping rodeo ride" on Babe.

As we approached the fence, we spotted Babe on the cow path down near the pond. We called her name, she turned her head, held it high in the air, and looked at us with her ears perked straight up. We called again, holding our apples high in the air hoping, I guess, that she could see them. For whatever reason, she came trotting up the path to the fence that we were all standing alongside of. I told the kids to let me give her my apple first. I held it over the top of the fence, calling her name, my arm fully extended with the apple in my hand. Slowly and cautiously Babe approached me, opened her mouth and took a bite, biting down on my fingers in the process, which hurt like the devil. The kids all laughed and showed me how to hold the apple in the flat of my hand in order to feed her. I told them I was going to climb the fence, and when I was ready, one of them was to call Babe over to the fence close to where I was sitting and when she was eating her apple, I would jump on her back and go for my ride. After that, we would get some more apples and do the same thing for each one of them until everyone had had their turn.

Cousin Dale managed to get Babe parallel to the fence post I was sitting on and at the right moment, off the post I slid and onto Babe's back, grabbing her mane in both my fists. Babe took off like a bullet fired from a gun, just like she did when she was turned loose and was freed from the truck the day she arrived. She was running like she was chasing some elusive calf and was determined to not let it get away. With each gallop, I tightened my grip in the hair of her mane and with each gallop I could feel myself sliding off to the right side of her back. I tightened my legs that were wrapped around her sides and belly but I knew the inevitable was about to happen. I was going to slide all the way around and fall off. She was flying down the cow path, her hooves pounding the dirt, and I was holding on to her mane with all of my might and squeezing her middle with all the strength in I had in my legs while thinking I was going to die. My brain told me that if the fall wasn't going to kill me, it would be her beating hooves that were going to crush the life out of me.

About a quarter of the way down the path, I slid all the way around her belly and fell to the ground covering my head with my hands and my face with my arms. The moment I hit the ground, Babe stopped dead in her tracks. I rolled out of the way and then she just walked a few paces away and turned sideways just looking at me before trotting off down to the bank of the pond. My cousins all came running to where I was laying on the ground asking if I was alright. They told me Babe stopped galloping just like roping horses make a dead stop in the rodeo, using their back legs to dig into the ground, before backing up to tighten the rope on the calf so the rider can jump off and tie up the calf's legs. For the moment, they were most impressed and I was their rodeo hero minus one rope and one calf.

We all walked back to the barn together and I said we need to get some more apples from the back room and who would like to be next? For some reason, no one else wanted a ride that day. The kids told Uncle George what happened that day and he just smiled and laughed a little under his breath. I don't think it was a big surprise for him how it all turned out.

Wearing of the Green

Francis Morris, my wife's father, was born and baptized on the same day, in a small Catholic Church on June 1, 1908, in Northern Ireland. We know this as a fact because many years ago, Charlotte and I spent the better part of two weeks in Ireland searching for her father's birth records. After almost giving up, we were able to locate the small village where the church is located that provided a copy of his Certificate of Birth and Baptism which we now have framed at our home. We also located the old foundation of his childhood home, and the still existing, well-kept two-room school building that he attended as a young lad.

Needless to explain, the wearing of the green, the symbol of Irish nationalism, and St. Paddy's Day, is close and dear to Charlotte's heart. Green, the adopted color of the Irish rebellion, as well as the shamrock, became the key symbols of the movement for a free Ireland. One of the motivating factors driving Frances Morris to emigrate to the United States was that, as a practicing Catholic and living in Northern Ireland, employment, government, and service sector positions were reserved only for Protestants and the same practice was the standard for Protestants when they tried to purchase land. They could not, simply because of their religious faith.

The green on the national flag symbolizes the Gaelic political and social order of Ireland. The green represents the Catholic side of the flag, while the orange on the flag symbolizes the followers of William of Orange in Ireland, or the Protestants. The white in the center of the flag signifies a lasting peace and hope for union between the Protestants and

Catholics in Ireland. With this as background, there was just a one and only time that I didn't wear green on a March day many years ago to honor St. Patrick and the Irish. Here is how it unfolded...

Not being Catholic, nor sensitive to history and traditions... actually being a jerk, I decided to not wear green, but to "split the difference" so to speak and wear a green sport jacket and an orange tie to school. After all, I reasoned at the time, I was a teacher in a high school that was overwhelmingly Italian and I thought it would be noticed by the students and they would find it somewhat silly, and besides, I doubted any student would have come from Irish heritage. How wrong could I have been?

The first hurdle for me to clear was leaving home that morning. As I picked up my briefcase, Charlotte called me back to the door as I was leaving. She had one of her hands behind her back...

"What do you need?"

"Come here for just a minute."

"OK... what's up?"

"I just want to give you a kiss before you leave."

I walked back, in love, very much looking forward to a sweet peck either on the cheek or from her warm sweet lips, and as I was ever so close, Charlotte's one hand reached up and grabbed the bottom of my orange tie, while at the same time, the other hand that was behind her back, reached up, holding a pair of scissors, and ever so neatly and quickly, sniped my entire tie in half. She handed me both tails and said ever so sweetly, "Love you, have a nice day!"

By the end of the school day, I realized that on St. Patrick's Day, everyone is Irish.

If a Little is Good...

As a guy who has always been fascinated with cars and all sorts of mechanical things, and one who has had much experience with building and repairing such wondrous things, I must admit, I've stepped into messes before and inadvertently tracked the mess across the rug, so to speak. Early on in my life, I was always attracted to historical, vintage, classic, automobiles, tractors and trucks, basically, all of which were of American manufactures.

My exposure to foreign produced automobiles was limited by several factors, some of which were, the automobile owner's circles I traveled in, where I lived, car magazines I read, and the fact that they were fairly rare and many were very limited by importation barriers and few foreign car dealerships, as well as few were sold to the car buying public. It wasn't until I was a teenager that a few German produced VWs and Mercedes were imported and dealerships were just starting to be established. Many of the foreign manufactured automobiles, so common today, were simply not seen, advertised, or for that matter, even existed here in the US.

For decades of ownership and driving, I've enjoyed automobiles manufactured in the US, with one exception, which happened to be our first new car, a 1961 VW 'bug.' It was with great interest that in the neighborhood where we had our first home and raised our children, that one of our friends always lusted for an Audi. He drove new Ramblers and Larks but lusted for an Audi and confided in me when pressed, that it just wasn't in his family budget. When employment benefits and salary improved, he moved on to owning new station wagons, fairly expensive, but still not as pricey as his dream car, an Audi. He then inherited an almost new Buick from his father-in-law's estate. Surely, I thought, with an extra car to use or sell, it was time to treat himself to his dream car, but it didn't happen. Life moved on, both our families moved on, but we stayed in touch and remained the best of friends.

Many years passed and we were living and working in the North Country, in a place called Parishville, to be specific. We had built a new home on the water and invited our friends to visit and join us for the weekend. All of us were excited to be together and catch up on the news of families and our lives in general. Now there is a reason why Parishville and the greater area is referred to as the North Country, and that is, it is very cold there in the winter. So cold in fact that I swear to you, the first snowflake to fall to the ground in November remains there until June. When we lived there, we remember one January when the red line on the thermometer on the porch never rose beyond the zero line. I'm not kidding you. For us, the word cold had a brand-new meaning as well as a new definition having grown up living in Rochester.

Our friends arrived late one Friday evening. It was dark and cold, and as I assisted in unloading the car, I couldn't help but notice the new car and that Jim was bursting with pride. He finally had his Audi! I never thought it would happen and perhaps Jim didn't think it would either, but there it was, glittering and shinning in our driveway as the wind was blowing and it was snowing. I told Jim that I was going to move my Ford Pinto out of the one side of our two-car garage and he should park his Audi in my spot. I had to insist and he reluctantly complied with unrelenting insistence.

We enjoyed the weekend together, shared meals, played cards, and chatted late into both Friday and Saturday evenings. Sunday morning, the thermometer was still hovering very close to zero. Breakfast discussion turned to Jim and Linda's plans for returning to Rochester later that day and thinking about going to work on Monday. Jim is a planner, in fact, that's what he was hired for at his manufacturing facility. After breakfast, he went out to just check on his love parked in the garage and, to his dismay, it was so cold in the garage it barely turned over when he tried to start it. He was worried that when it came time to leave later that afternoon, he wouldn't be able to start his Audi. I told him I had the perfect solution and he had total faith and confidence in me given I was a car guy and on top of that, a science guy.

Trusting me was mistake number one for Jim. Mistake number two for Jim was my proposed solution. Part of our heating system we relied on to heat our home was the use of a wood burning stove. So I told Jim, about a half an hour before he wanted to leave, I would take some hot ashes out of the stove, put them in a metal tray I had, carry them out to the garage, place the tray under the engine, and it would warm up the engine quickly. Well, I'm one of those folks who believe in the school of thought that if a little if good, more is better. Mistake number three, not Jim's, but mine! My thinking, or lack thereof, went something like this: it was very cold in the garage, the pan of ashes will sit on the cold concrete floor absorbing much of the heat, the ashes will quickly cool off, so logically, the use of more hot embers will be so much better to give off the heat needed to warm up the cold engine. My brilliant plan was to be executed exactly one-half hour before departure time, and so it was.

Jim and I walked out to the garage together and he slid into the front seat behind the steering wheel. Jim inserted the key into the switch, turned it, and the car started like it was on the beach in sunny Florida in the middle of July. Perfect! I was grinning and ever so proud of my idea. Jim and Linda were also impressed. We said our goodbyes, shared our hugs, and waved as they backed out of the driveway, pulled away, and headed down the road.

Later that evening, actually very late that evening the phone rang. It was Jim calling from Syracuse.

Jim's sad voice on the other end said, "Hi, just wanted to let you know we've had car trouble just in case you tried calling us at home and we didn't answer."

"Oh no, what happened?"

"I don't know, the engine oil light came on and I stopped driving immediately."

"Where did this happen?"

"On 81, just before the thruway entrance in Syracuse."

"Where are you now?"

"We had the car towed to the Audi dealership in Syracuse."

"OK, I'll leave right now and come and pick you up and drive you to Rochester."

"No need to do that, I called our next-door neighbor before I called you and he's on his way right now. We'll won't know anything until tomorrow when the dealership opens up and the mechanics take a look and see if they can identify the problem with the engine."

"OK, you sure you're set?"

"I'll call you tomorrow after I find out what the dealer tells me what the problem is and what they need to do to correct it."

I went to bed, thinking about Jim's Audi and why I never liked foreign automobiles and the bad luck Jim was having with his dream car. After all these years, he finally has an opportunity and finances to purchase an Audi, and now on his first trip, he didn't even make it back home. I fell asleep thinking, it's an Audi, what would one expect other than problems and reliability, and how sad I felt for Jim. The next day, Monday evening Jim called.

"Hi Gary, Jim here"

"What did the mechanics find out, what did they say, and what needs to be done to fix the problem?"

"The dealership said as best as they could figure out, the oil pan gasket failed and all the oil in the engine leaked out as I drove from Parishville to Syracuse. They said it was a good thing I stopped when I did or I would have totally ruined the engine. They are going to have to replace all the gaskets in the oil pan and in the bottom of the engine. I should have the car back by the end of the week."

"What will it cost you?"

"I don't know yet. We are trying to figure out what's covered under the warranty"

"What about the towing?"

"That will all be covered by AAA, thank goodness."

"Jim, you might not want to tell the dealership about the tray. I'm thinking the heat dried up or shrank the gaskets allowing all the engine oil to leak out. My fault, I didn't think it all the way through. I am sorry."

Jim owned his dream car for two weeks after driving it home from the Syracuse dealership where he had it repaired. He traded it in on a new car and it wasn't another Audi.

More is not always... better.

She was a Beauty and it was My Birthday After All

The DeKay family was a wild bunch that lived down in the hollow on a dirt road past and below where the schoolhouse was located. From the hard top road, one could see down the dirt road which served as a sort of driveway to DeKay's old, and not well-maintained, house and barn. A 1920s John Deer tractor, hay wagon, plows, drags, and mowing machine were haphazardly parked around and near the barn while old cars and broken-down trucks were parked where they died, and for sure, had no hope of a resuscitation. The ones that still had some life in them and were running were parked among the lifeless hulks, awaiting who knows what?

On this one special summer's day in July, I could not ignore the brand new 1956 Ford parked among the battered and bruised carcasses of former Detroit's glamor chariots from years gone by. I was one of the first observers to notice the out-of-place red and white two-tone Ford Crown Victoria hardtop. The gleaming chrome strip over the roof, accentuating the classic lines of this newly released model, added a richness to the red and white colors of the body. I had to know more about this phenomenon as no one around here could possibly own a vehicle like this one, particularly the DeKays.

I was a playmate and friend of the kids in the family, as I spent summers on the neighboring farm which belonged to my aunt and uncle. DeKay's small farm consisted of perhaps 20 acres. Chet DeKay tried his hand at raising some livestock and crops of hay and corn to feed his cattle during the winter months, but success in this area was difficult to come by. Chet's main income was derived by factory work during the week at the Ingersoll Rand plant in Dansville, several miles away. As for the family, Jimmy was two years younger than I was at 16, his sister Pat was my age, and her older sister Marjorie was 18. Pat, or Patty, was my buddy. We laughed a lot, played tricks together on Jimmy and Marjorie for which they didn't appreciate our creative humor and basically wrote us off and out of their lives. But the Ford drew me back in to Marjorie's life web.

From day one, when I first noticed the Ford, it usually appeared around two o'clock in the afternoon, was never there in the morning, and seemed to disappear about one o'clock in the morning. It was never dusty or dirty; on the contrary, it gleamed with fresh coats of wax every Monday. I found my way down to see Patty and inquire about the new car. She told me it belonged to Marjorie's new boyfriend, who also worked with her dad at the plant, and that they rode together to work. The boyfriend lived in the next town down old Route 10 in Cameron, and he drove up to DeKays every day to ride to work with Patty's dad. That is why the car appeared and disappeared on a regular schedule. Patty told me Chet had put in a good word for Marjorie's boyfriend and that is why he got the job at the plant. The factory paid an excellent wage and hence, the reason the new car appeared at the DeKays making Marjorie very happy. The future for Marjorie and her new boyfriend seemed bright and they planned their marriage later in the year.

As I recall, it was near my birthday in early August when I went to visit Patty and share some birthday cake that she and her mom had baked for me. We spent the evening chatting, having cake, and then the inevitable question...

Patty	"What are we going to do tonight?"
Me	"I don't know."
Patty	"There's a dance at the hall in Jasper tonight, want to go?"
Me	"Sure, but how we gonna get there?"

Patty shouting to her sister in the other room...

Patty	"Marjorie, want to go to the Square dance at the hall in Jasper tonight?"
Marjorie	"Where?"
Patty	"You know, the place over in Jasper. They have a live band and a caller."
Marjorie	"Sounds like fun! How we gonna get there?"
Patty	"We can take your boyfriend's car."
Marjorie	"You know I can't drive a standard shift."
Patty	"Gary can drive. Gary, you can drive, right? You know how to drive a standard."
Me	"Sure!"
Marjorie	"Will you be very careful with the new Ford"
Me	"Sure will! You can count on me; I'll be super careful."
Patty	"Marjorie, what do you say? Gary can drive and we are all set. Besides, what are we gonna do if we just hang around here all night when we can have a great time at the dance?"

Marjorie	"I don't know... I'm nervous."
Patty	"What are you afraid of? We'll park his car exactly where he parked it when we get back and no one else will ever know the difference. We'll put gas in it to fill it up to exactly the same spot on the gas gauge. Come on Marjorie, it's Gary's birthday; let's have some fun!"
Marjorie	"OK, BUT we need to park it in the same spot, put gas in it, and take the back roads so no one sees us."
Patty	"Deal. Let's go!"

All the back roads were dirt or gravel and over hills and dales to where the dance hall was located. We drove miles, got lost a few times, and eventually made it there, parking a mile away and walking the rest of the way hoping no one would see us or notice the car off the road in the woods in the farmer's wood lot. We enjoyed the fiddler, danced a few sets, laughed a lot and finally realized it was getting late and we had to find a gas station that was still open. We didn't see anyone we recognized at the dance, thank goodness!

On the way home we thought about where to get gas and realized the only place near us was the general store in Cameron. Cameron! That's where the boyfriend lived. Our only other chance was the town of Bath, miles away. No choice, we had to make a run for it and take the back roads all the way. It was a thrilling trip! The new Ford had the biggest engine one could order. It was powerful!

We slid around corners on the gravel, spinning the tires all the way, and laughing until we had tears in our eyes. Marjorie was enjoying this more than we were. I don't know what she was thinking or what she was feeling, but we all were having a wonderful time packed together in the front seat, sliding around on the seat on all the sharp corners we were taking at a speed that wasn't prudent.

We found a gas station in Bath that was still open and spent the last five dollars we had between us filling the tank up to the proper mark on the gauge. We repeated the return trip on the same type of roads, driving too fast, and sliding around corners, trying to make sure we could see the road and the corners in time before we outran the distance shown by the headlights. The car was dusty and dirty when we got back to the house. We inspected the car and determined we had no choice but to wash it and dry it!

We drove it out to the barnyard, carried buckets of soapy water from the kitchen and gave it a thorough cleaning and wash. Returning from the kitchen with buckets of rinse water, the chrome sparkled and the red and white waxed paint reflected the moonlight perfectly! We carefully wiped the car down with all the kitchen dishtowels we could find and parked it perfectly in its original spot. No one thought about the odometer, but alas, no one was ever the wiser. Our luck continued.

Marjorie and her boyfriend broke up that fall during hunting season. I took my driver's test after I got my permit later that August after returning to Rochester and the beginning of the new school year.

Woven Tapestry

It is interesting how the tapestry of life is woven from circumstances, events, and people we interact with during the time we spend on our earthly journey. This tale reflects just a few of my many naive and poor decisions, and (let's be honest) embarrassing and shameful actions encountered on my journey, many of my own making.

We had just purchased our first home in a new housing development, you know, the dream corner lot, big yard, white picket fence... really, that was what it was. And what it turned out to be. At the time, I was teaching in the City of Rochester, living in the burbs. We thought it was the ideal life and couldn't be any better given our "roots." The buzz of the neighborhood was what was going on in the school district where the kids of our neighborhood all attended. During this time, the teachers' union and the district apparently could not reach an agreement for a new contract and the "issues" were somehow showing their ugliness in the local newspapers as well as in the classrooms, or so we thought. Friends and neighbors thought we needed to do something, anything, to resolve the conflict and silly me, I raised my hand.

So the way I thought I would get involved and try to handle this was to start at the top of the pyramid. I called the Superintendent of the school district, a Mr. Joseph Clement and told him that I represented the parents of the Cross Gates community, and we would like to meet with him to discuss the apparent impasse in teacher negotiations. He agreed to a meeting at our home and we set a date and time. I left him with the assumption it would be us, a married couple, and maybe a few other parents that would be meeting with him. The meeting information was shared with the neighborhood and everyone wanted in on the meeting with the superintendent and so, without thinking too deeply about all the implications, or issue of fairness regarding the superintendent, they were all invited. On said date, our kitchen, dining and living rooms were bursting with our neighbors, I'd guess twenty or more. All were invited to gather fifteen minutes before the time Mr. Clement was scheduled to arrive. Since this was a neighborhood meeting, everyone walked and no automobiles were parked in the driveway or on the roadway, looking totally innocent enough, but still a set-up.

Right on time, a Buick pulled up in front of our home and three gentlemen stepped out. The doorbell rang, and I welcomed them into the living room. We would out later find out from introductions the superintendent, Mr. Joseph Clement, the assistant superintendent, Dr. Robert Sudlow, and the president of the board, Mr. William C. Munn were meeting with us. Our guests were surprised by the number of folks packed into our home, but they were calm, cool and collected. The team answered all our questions about what was going on in the district and took time to explain the district's position on the costs of items being proposed in the new contract and a bit about the process of how negotiations are conducted.

Negotiations dragged on for months and no agreement or contract was forthcoming. The new buzz in the neighborhood was we needed to have representation on the board of education. I raised my hand again outlining conditions that friends and neighbors would get all the necessary signatures on the petition, that they would pass out flyers before election going door-to-door. They agreed and worked hard and I was elected.

The Taylor Law governing teacher negotiations had just recently been passed by the NYS Legislature and a teacher serving on a board was a 'new thing' or new twist. Articles were written in newspapers and union magazines regarding the question, could or should a teacher serve on a board of education and could he or she be 'fair' and not just represent the teachers' point of view or self-interests? I could feel the pressure of being under the microscope and being watched to see where I stood on all major issues related to finances, teacher salaries, benefits, and contract negotiations.

At the first board meeting, I was given time to speak by members of the board and asked what I had hoped to accomplish as a new member. I made a statement something to the effect that I was here to do what's best for the boys and girls of the district and that I was not a politician nor interested in being one. After the board meeting ended, Bill Munn asked if I could stay a few minutes to have cup of coffee and chat. I agreed. I found out that Bill, the board present, was a well-respected salesman and beloved by all. He had a magnetic personality and was the antithesis of Willy Loman in Death of a Salesman.

Bill Munn knew all the best places in the state to find the stores and stands that served the best ice cream. This inside information served me well for many years. Bill also shared his thoughts and insights with me which proved to be a truism over many years, and it was this: unless I learned to be a politician, I would never be able to achieve anything. He told me that from his point of view, politics is not a bad thing, it is how things get done. Politics, he explained, is understanding the other persons' points of view and then merging ides and working together to accomplish some common goals. My coffee got cold that evening and I went home with a lot on my mind to think about.

A few months passed and I remember always having to comment on presentations that Dr. Sudlow made regarding anything to do with curriculum. My comments usually related to a focus on learner-center education and meeting student needs and learning styles. After several of these unscripted comments at many meetings, Mr. Clement had had enough. He picked up his pipe, banged it on the ash tray in front of him, knocking out all the ashes and blurted out,

"Buehler, if you're so damn smart, why aren't you a superintendent?"

Once again, I went home with a lot on my mind. Over my years on the board, I was privileged to have served both as vice president and then president during my three elected terms. Life moved on and I moved on with my career. I worked in several administrative positions in central office in the Rochester CSD. Over time, I was fortunate to have served as superintendent in four NYS districts and then the weaving of the tapestry began in earnest. Old friends reappeared in my life in interesting ways, bringing to mind the many naive and poor decisions of past decades.

Fast forward twenty-five years and I was living in another part of the state when I learned that Bill Munn was being treated for cancer. Upon his passing, and soon after, the board renamed a school in the Spencerport school district, the William C. Munn Elementary School. I couldn't help myself but to reflect on our very first meeting and the cold cup of coffee. If had accomplished anything in my life, was it by being a politician and did I do it by trying to understand the other persons' points of view and then merging ideas and working together to accomplish our common goals? The weaving of the tapestry continued.

I was working in the Oswego City district when the assistant superintendent for business had a wonderful offer for a position in Syracuse and asked me if I would support him as an applicant. Of course, the answer was 'yes' regardless of the fact that it was in the middle of budget preparation and the timing was terrible as it was the spring of the year. Mike was successful in his quest, which left the district in a difficult position, with regards to timing and the recruitment of an experienced finance administrator as well as being faced by the challenging task of budget development and completion. I called my old friend Joe Clement (the one you remember that said, Buehler if you know so much...) and asked him how his retirement in Florida was going. After some chit-chat, I asked Joe how he felt about coming north for a few weeks to give me a hand and help out a bit with the budget. I suggested that it might be exciting for him to 'get back in the saddle' for a ride and that he might enjoy the 'rodeo.'

He thought it would be a fun challenge, took me up on my offer, and Joe and I worked together in a different capacity from all those many years previously. Interestingly, weeks turned into months, not only for the rest of that school year, but he stayed on for another six months the following year. And yes, the budget passed with flying colors and the board was very pleased with his knowledge, skills, and work. The weaving of the tapestry continued for a few more years.

I retired from the district after thirty-five years in education and was offered a visiting professorship at SUNY Oswego which lasted five years. I was then offered a core faculty position with Union which demanded much of my attention for eight additional years. During this period of time, one of my Ph.D. students needed some assistance and was searching for a new member for his dissertation committee. I suggested that he may wish to call Dr. Robert Sudlow to ask him if he would consider joining his committee and once again, the retired superintendent for curriculum from the Spencerport school district and I were working together. I never mentioned to him during our time together anything about learner-centered education, for you see, he was one of our nation's leading authorities on effective schools. I still wonder what was going through his mind when I spoke up at those board meetings decades earlier?

The sad fact of life is we don't get 'do overs' in weaving life's tapestry, but we can learn from our mistakes, naivete and poor judgements, decisions, embarrassing and shameful actions on the journey.

When I take a quick glance in the rearview mirror, I can't contain myself from laughing out loud now that I see how the tapestry is woven.

www.ingramcontent.com/pod-product-compliance
Lightning Source LLC
Chambersburg PA
CBHW021504090426
42739CB00007B/458